Peter Adamson and the University of St Andrews.

Seamus Heaney

A photograph taken during Seamus Heaney's visit to the University of St. Andrews in October 1999 to give a reading in memory of the late Dr. George Jack of the University's School of English.

SEAMUS HEANEY

Second Edition

ANDREW MURPHY

Northcote House
in association with the
British Council

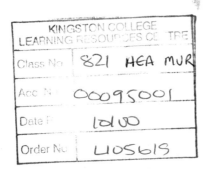
First published 1996
Second edition 2000

First published in 1996 by Northcote House Publishers Ltd,
Horndon House, Horndon, Tavistock, Devon, PL19 9NQ,
United Kingdom.
Tel: +44 (01822) 810066 Fax: +44 (01822) 810034.

British Library Cataloguing in Publication Data
A catalogue record for this book is available from the British Library

ISBN 0-7463-0962-7

Typeset by Florence Productions Ltd, Stoodleigh, Devon
Printed and bound in Great Britain by
The Baskerville Press Ltd, Salisbury, Wiltshire, SP2 7QB

In memory of
Andrew Michael
1926–1998

Contents

Acknowledgements

In the first edition of this study I expressed my gratitude to Eibhlín Evans, Geraldine Higgins and John Lucas for their very helpful comments on my manuscript. It gives me great pleasure to thank them here again. I also extend my thanks now to Neil Corcoran for his helpful feedback. As ever, I am deeply indebted to Gerard Murphy and Charonne Ruth for their unfailing support. Finally, my publishers and I are grateful to Seamus Heaney and Faber and Faber Ltd for permission to quote from the works of Seamus Heaney.

The cover photograph of Seamus Heaney is by courtesy of Peter Adamson and the University of St. Andrews. It was taken during Seamus Heaney's visit to the University in October 1999, to give a reading in memory of the late Dr. George Jack of the University's School of English.

Biographical Outline

1939   Born 13 April, the eldest of nine children. Family home is the farm 'Mossbawn', in County Derry, Northern Ireland.

1945–51   Attends the local Anahorish School.

1947   UK Education Act makes extended education more accessible to the children of less-well-off families. In Northern Ireland, specifically, opens up educational opportunities for Catholics.

1951–7   Attends, as a boarder, St Columb's College, Derry. Among the other graduates of St Columb's are the nationalist politician John Hume, left-wing journalist Eamonn McCann, literary critic and poet Seamus Deane, and the playwright Brian Friel.

1953   Family moves from 'Mossbawn' to a nearby farm called 'The Wood', which Heaney's father had inherited from an uncle. At about this time, Heaney's 4-year-old brother, Christopher, is killed in a road accident – an incident which the poet writes about in 'Mid-Term Break'.

1957–61   Attends Queen's University, Belfast. Graduates with 1st class degree in English Language and Literature. Is urged to undertake postgraduate work at Oxford, but decides to become a school teacher instead.

1961–2   Attends St Joseph's College of Education, Andersonstown, Belfast, and obtains his Teacher's Training Diploma. During his time at St Joseph's, Heaney writes an extended essay on Northern Irish literary magazines and encounters the work of local poets such as John Hewitt.

1962	Joins staff of St Thomas's Intermediate School, Ballymurphy, Belfast. The headmaster is the short-story writer Michael McLaverty, who introduces Heaney to the work of the Irish poet Patrick Kavanagh.
1962–3	Part-time postgraduate work at Queen's.
1963–6	Teaches at St Joseph's College of Education.
1963	Philip Hobsbaum establishes Belfast Group. Members include: Michael Longley, Stewart Parker, and James Simmons.
1965	August: marries Marie Devlin. Devlin was born in Ardboe in County Tyrone. She attended St Mary's College of Education in Belfast from 1958 to 1962 and taught at St Columcille's school in County Down.
1966	*Death of a Naturalist* published. Hobsbaum moves to Glasgow; Heaney joins Queen's faculty. Belfast Group continues to meet at Heaney's and includes younger members such as Paul Muldoon, Frank Ormsby, and Michael Foley. July: Heaneys' son Michael born.
1967	Heaney receives the Somerset Maugham Award.
1968	February: second son, Christopher, born. Receives the Cholmondeley Award.
1968–9	Repression of Civil Rights movement prompts a renewal of conflict in Northern Ireland.
1969	*Door into the Dark* published. August: British troops deployed in Derry and Belfast.
1970–1	Teaches as guest lecturer at University of California, Berkeley.
1971	August: internment introduced in Northern Ireland. By the end of the year, a total of 1,576 people have been imprisoned without benefit of trial.
1972	30 January, 'Bloody Sunday': soldiers from the British Army paratroop regiment open fire on unarmed Civil Rights demonstrators in Derry. Thirteen protesters are killed, a further twelve are wounded. August: the Heaneys move to Glanmore, in the Republic of Ireland. Makes his first attempts at translating the medieval Irish poem *Buile Suibhne*. November: *Wintering Out* published.
1973	April: daughter, Catherine Ann, born.

1975	*North* published. Receives the W. H. Smith Award and Duff Cooper Prize. October: joins faculty of Carysfort Teacher Training College.
1976	November: Heaney and family move to Sandymount, near Dublin.
1979	*Field Work* published. Spends a term at Harvard University as one of a series of temporary successors to the American poet Robert Lowell.
1980	*Preoccupations*, his first collection of essays, published. *Selected Poems 1965–1975* published.
1980–1	Nationalist prisoners in Northern Ireland stage a series of hunger strikes, seeking the reintroduction of political (as opposed to criminal) status. Ten prisoners would eventually die on the protest, including Francis Hughes of Bellaghy, near Heaney's birthplace.
1981	Leaves Carysfort.
1982	January: starts a five-year contract at Harvard, to teach one semester a year. Publishes (as co-editor with Ted Hughes) an anthology of poems entitled *The Rattle Bag*.
1983	*An Open Letter* published as a pamphlet by Field Day in Ireland. The verse letter objects to his work being included in an anthology of British poetry. His translation of *Buile Suibhne*, entitled *Sweeney Astray*, is published in Ireland.
1984	*Station Island* published. *Sweeney Astray* published in the UK. Elected to Boylston Chair of Rhetoric and Oratory at Harvard. October: mother dies.
1986	October: father dies.
1987	*Haw Lantern* published. Receives the Whitbread Award.
1988	*Government of the Tongue*, his second collection of essays, published. Becomes Professor of Poetry at Oxford University (for a term of five years).
1990	*The Cure at Troy*, Heaney's version of Sophocles' *Philoctetes*, performed in Derry and published in London. *New Selected Poems* published.
1991	*Seeing Things* published.
1994	First round of ceasefires in Northern Ireland (August).
1995	October: Heaney awarded the Nobel Prize for Literature. *Redress of Poetry* published.

1996	*The Spirit Level* published. Heaney receives Commonwealth Award. Resigns as Boylston Professor at Harvard, to become Emerson Poet in Residence. IRA ceasefire terminated (February).
1997	*Spirit Level* named Whitbread Book of the Year. IRA ceasefire renewed (July).
1998	*Opened Ground: Poems 1966–1996* published. 'Good Friday' Agreement signed by British and Irish governments and by most Northern Irish political parties, including Sinn Féin and the Ulster Unionist Party (April).
1999	Heaney's translation of *Beowulf* published.
2000	*Beowulf* receives the Whitbread Poetry Award.

Abbreviations

B.   *Beowulf* (London: Faber & Faber, 1999)

CT   *The Cure at Troy* (London: Faber & Faber, 1990)

DD   *Door into the Dark* (London: Faber & Faber, 1969)

DN   *Death of a Naturalist* (London: Faber & Faber, 1966)

FW   *Field Work* (London: Faber & Faber, 1979)

GT   *The Government of the Tongue: The 1986 T. S. Eliot Memorial Lectures and Other Critical Writings* (London: Faber & Faber, 1988)

HL   *The Haw Lantern* (London: Faber & Faber, 1987)

N.   *North* (London: Faber & Faber, 1975)

OG   *Opened Ground: Poems 1966–1996* (London: Faber & Faber, 1998)

OL   'An Open Letter', in *Ireland's Field Day* (Notre Dame: University of Notre Dame Press, 1986)

P.   *Preoccupations: Selected Prose 1968–1978* (London: Faber & Faber, 1980)

RP   *The Redress of Poetry: Oxford Lectures* (London: Faber & Faber, 1996)

SA   *Sweeney Astray* (London: Faber & Faber, 1984)

SI   *Station Island* (London: Faber & Faber, 1984)

SL   *The Spirit Level* (London: Faber & Faber, 1996)

ST   *Seeing Things* (London: Faber & Faber, 1991)

WO   *Wintering Out* (London: Faber & Faber, 1972)

I come from scraggy farm and moss,
Old patchworks that the pitch and toss
Of history have left dishevelled.

('A Peacock's Feather', *The Haw Lantern*)

Introduction

Humming
Solders all broken hearts. Death's edge
Blunts on the narcotic strumming.

(Seamus Heaney, 'The Folk Singers' (*DN* 42))

Seamus Heaney begins his second collection of prose writings, *The Government of the Tongue*, with a prefatory essay entitled 'The Interesting Case of Nero, Chekhov's Cognac and a Knocker'. He opens the essay with a telling anecdote. In 1972, he says, he had arranged to meet the singer David Hammond in Belfast in order to go to the BBC studios in the city and put together a tape of songs and poems for a mutual friend of theirs, living in Michigan. In the event, the tape did not get made. As Hammond and Heaney made their way to the studios, the city was rocked by a series of explosions. The air filled with the sound of the sirens of emergency vehicles converging on the city centre. Heaney tells us

> It was music against which the music of the guitar that David unpacked made little impression. So little, indeed, that the very notion of beginning to sing at that moment when others were beginning to suffer seemed like an offence against their suffering. He could not raise his voice at that cast-down moment. He packed the guitar again and we both drove off into the destroyed evening. (*GT*, p. xi)

It is no surprise that Heaney should choose to preface his book with an account of this incident. Reflected in the story, we find some of the central concerns which have both motivated and troubled the poet's career as a writer. Some of these conflicts Heaney himself makes explicit as he proceeds through the essay. Central among them are what Heaney notes as the conflicting demands of art and life, or, put another way, of song and suffering. On the day in question, Heaney tells us, he and Hammond had felt that their art of song and poetry was

1

simply silenced in the face of the suffering occasioned by the brutal scenes taking shape outside the studio walls. 'What David Hammond and I were experiencing, at a most immediate and obvious level,' he tells us, 'was a feeling that song constituted a betrayal of suffering' (*GT*, p. xii).

In the course of his prefatory essay, and in the pieces that follow it in *The Government of the Tongue*, Heaney comes to revise this view, at least in the sense of rendering it more complex, and seeking to map out a place for poetry in the face of suffering. He both endorses and feels endorsed by the philosophy of the Polish poet, Zbigniew Herbert (who had himself suffered the oppressions of Soviet-dominated Poland), whose poem 'A Knocker' Heaney summarizes as a deceptively simple statement: ' "Go in peace," his poem says. "Enjoy poetry as long as you don't use it to escape reality" ' (*GT*, pp. xviii–xix). Through Herbert, Heaney seeks to strike a delicate balance: between the poet's responsibility to the artifice of his or her own creation and the poet's responsibility to his or her immediate political, historical, and social world.

We might say that Heaney's career has been characterized by a continual negotiation between the various responsibilities of the poet delineated here. Patrick Kavanagh, a fellow Irish poet (whose work greatly influenced Heaney's), once observed of poetry that 'a man . . . innocently dabbles in words and rhymes and finds that it is his life. Versing activity leads him away from the paths of conventional unhappiness.'[1] In Heaney's case, however, we might say that we encounter an instance of a poet who embarks on a literary career dabbling in a certain kind of words and rhymes, dedicated to a certain range of subject matter, but who, as his career progresses, increasingly finds certain political and historical considerations impinging upon him, demanding that he engage with them within the arena of his work. While, at a personal level, poetry may well have led him 'away from the paths of conventional unhappiness', in time historical and political circumstances inevitably led him back to confront a very profound kind of unhappiness: the unhappiness of injustice and loss, of individual and communal grief. In more specific terms, we might say that Heaney begins his career by fashioning himself as a poet very much in the mould of Kavanagh: a poet concerned with what Heaney

2

himself has called, in discussing Kavanagh, 'the unregarded data of the usual life' (GT 7). Like Kavanagh, Heaney set out as a poet seeking both to celebrate and to scrutinize the contours of such a life. As a Catholic growing up and living in the Protestant-dominated Northern Ireland statelet, however, political considerations very frequently pulled at the fabric of the 'usual life' that Heaney experienced, ultimately straining it to breaking point.[2]

A poem such as 'A Constable Calls' from Heaney's fourth volume, North, allusively registers the subtle ways in which Heaney's community was subjected, as part of its experience of day-to-day life, to a system of power from which its members felt alienated. At first reading, the poem seems to trace a relatively genial, bureaucratic visit to the Heaneys' farm by a local police constable. On closer inspection, however, we find that throughout the poem there runs a note of fear of the policeman's authority, and the poem's vocabulary persistently carries an ominous note of the brutal force held available to be exercised by this agent of the state (the dynamo on the policeman's bicycle is 'cocked back', like the hammer of a gun; the bicycle's pedals are momentarily 'relieved | Of the boot of the law'; most explicitly, the child narrator stares at 'the polished holster | With its buttoned flap, the braid cord | Looped into the revolver butt' (N. 60)). In the final image of the poem, we are told that, leaving the farm, the policeman's 'boot pushed off | And the bicycle ticked, ticked, ticked' (N. 61). As the poem closes, then, the ticking hub of the bicycle wheel conjures up an image of the timing device of a bomb, ticking its way down to the moment of explosion.

In a way, we can say that that ominous repetitive ticking of an explosion waiting to happen runs quietly but persistently through Heaney's early career as a poet. Though, in his first two published volumes, Heaney mostly preoccupies himself with a Kavanagh-inspired engagement with 'the unregarded data of the usual life', both volumes contain a small number of poems which advert in some way to the situation in Northern Ireland. As the 1960s drew to a close, a radical change occurred in the 'usual life' that formed the clearest focal point of Heaney's poetic vision in that decade. The anticipated explosion came at the turn of the decade when the Northern state finally collapsed

3

into continuous crisis, and the conflict in the province intensified and became progressively more and more bloody. At mid-career, Heaney found himself expected – and expecting himself – to address that crisis in his poetry. In *Wintering Out* (1972), *North* (1975), and *Field Work* (1979), Heaney returns again and again to the contemporary political situation, seeking ways to address it, to confront it in his work.

In a sense, then, having started his career in the manner of a Patrick Kavanagh, Heaney, at mid-career, found himself cast in something like the role of another Irish predecessor poet: W. B. Yeats. In 'Among School Children', Yeats describes himself as 'A sixty-year-old smiling public man',[3] and, as the situation in his homeland progressively deteriorated, Heaney too found himself thrust into the role of a public figure. His discomfort at his new high-profile status is registered in 'Exposure', placed at the very end of *North*:

> How did I end up like this?
> I often think of my friends'
> Beautiful prismatic counselling
> And the anvil brains of some who hate me
>
> As I sit weighing and weighing
> My responsible *tristia*.

> (*N*. 66)

Just as Yeats struggled to come to terms with another moment of crisis in Ireland in poems like 'September 1913', 'Easter 1916', 'The Rose Tree', and 'Meditations in Time of Civil War', so Heaney struggled to find an adequate way of addressing the conflicts of his particular historical moment in the poems he wrote and published from the early 1970s to the mid-1980s. Again like Yeats, he not only struggled to find expression for and poetic engagement with the political crisis, but also worried over the question of the nature of the poet's responsibility to that political situation.[4] What, both men wondered, was the role of the poet in and towards such times of crisis? In both men we find an anxiety concerning the relationship between the contemplative, essentially passive life of the poet and the active life of those who become directly involved in the affairs of the world. The point is made most forcefully by Yeats, perhaps, in his poem 'In Memory of Major Robert Gregory'. Killed in air combat in the

First World War, Gregory is the epitome for Yeats of the informed, self-conscious man of action:

> Some burn damp faggots, others may consume
> The entire combustible world in one small room
> As though dried straw, and if we turn about
> The bare chimney is gone black out
> Because the work had finished in that flare.
> Soldier, scholar, horseman, he,
> As 'twere all life's epitome.
> What made us dream that he could comb grey hair?[5]

By contrast with the brightly burning flame of the engaged, active life, the smokey 'damp faggots' nourished by the isolated poet may seem absurdly irrelevant, casting a pitifully wan light upon the world.

By the time Heaney came to publish *The Government of the Tongue* in 1988, however, he had made his peace with many of these issues. His rendering of Herbert's 'A Knocker' is indicative of how this accommodation has been reached: ' "Go in peace," his poem says. "Enjoy poetry as long as you don't use it to escape reality." ' The poet, in other words, must walk a fine line between commitment to the formal, aesthetic pleasures of the text and commitment to the social and political world in which the poem is composed, neglecting neither, acknowledging the force of both.

The desire to hold such contradictory impulses together is entirely characteristic of the later phase of Heaney's career. Take *The Government of the Tongue*, for instance. On the one hand, as Heaney himself notes, the title of this volume indicates the 'aspect of poetry as its own vindicating force. In this dispensation, the tongue (representing both a poet's personal gift of utterance and the common resources of language itself) has been granted the right to govern' (*GT* 92). On the other hand, he notes, 'my title can also imply a *denial* of the tongue's autonomy and permission. In this reading, "the government of the tongue" is full of monastic and ascetic strictness' (*GT* 96). Following on from the logic of this latter proposition, Heaney finds himself asking 'What right has poetry to its quarantine? Should it not put the governors on its joy and moralize its song?' (*GT* 99). The phrase 'the government of the tongue' thus holds together in fragile unity these two opposing positions (the right of poetry to an aesthetic autonomy; the necessity of subordinating poetry to political or moral constraints) and it is to just such a fragile unity that Heaney pledges fidelity.

We find the same doubleness in the title of Heaney's 1991 collection of poems, *Seeing Things*, which posits a visionary power in poetry, enabling us to '[squint] out from a skylight of the world' (*ST* 57), to achieve 'a pitch | | Beyond our usual hold upon ourselves' (*ST* 86). And yet, even as poetry allows us to achieve this transcendent vision, to 'see things' as we have not seen them before, the title also acts as a kind of brake on the possibility of our granting blind allegiance to such transcendent envisioning. As the title warns us, such transcendent sight may be no more than simply 'seeing things' – a self-deception in thinking we perceive what in fact does not exist at all. It is on this thin line between faith and scepticism that Heaney balances his later poetry.

Heaney himself ends the article with which we began this introduction by quoting from one of his own poems – 'The Singer's House', written for David Hammond. In the concluding stanza of the poem, Heaney writes:

> When I came here first you were always singing,
> a hint of the clip of the pick
> in your winnowing climb and attack.
> Raise it again, man. We still believe what we hear.
>
> (*GT*, p. xxiii; *FW* 27)

The poem was written in the wake of the abortive Belfast recording session which had been planned with Hammond. In a sense, it registers Heaney's ultimate belief in the necessity and value of the poetic act – his belief that, perhaps they ought, after all, to have continued with the session, despite the horrific events taking place outside the studio walls. But it is a hard-won belief. As he writes elsewhere in *The Government of the Tongue*:

> Here is the great paradox of poetry and of the imaginative arts in general. Faced with the brutality of the historical onslaught, they are practically useless. . . . In one sense the efficacy of poetry is nil – no lyric has ever stopped a tank. In another sense, it is unlimited. It is like the writing in the sand in the face of which accusers and accused are left speechless and renewed. (*GT* 107)

This complex view neatly indicates the trajectory of Heaney's career as a poet. His early faith in poetry is unconflicted. He revels in what he calls the 'primitive delight in finding world become word' (*GT* 8). In mid-career, he is brought into confrontation with 'the brutality of the historical onslaught' and struggles with the question of how he might encounter it in his work. The effect of this encounter is ultimately to renew his faith in poetry, but that faith is now tempered by a knowledge of poetry's desperate limitations; by a recognition that the transcendence that poetry offers is never more than tentative – an inscription in the sand that the incoming tide will surely obliterate. But, for all that, the force of poetry is still valid, still, in some fragile way, efficacious, so that, as Heaney puts it in *The Redress of Poetry*, it is possible 'to advance poetry beyond the point where it has been helping us to enjoy life to that even more profoundly verifying point where it helps us also to endure it' (*RP* 185), thus as he says in 'The Singer's House': 'We *still* believe what we hear.' Possibly we do not believe with quite the same innocent conviction as might once have been possible, but we do still believe.

1

'Living roots awaken in my head': Place and Displacement

Seamus Heaney first began publishing his poems during his time as an undergraduate at Queen's University in Belfast, when a number of pieces by him appeared in various student magazines. In 1963 he became a member of Philip Hobsbaum's 'Belfast Group', an informal gathering of young writers who would meet regularly at Hobsbaum's Belfast home to critique each other's work. Hobsbaum greatly admired Heaney's poetry and he exercized his influence to secure Heaney an entry into the London publishing world.[1] Through these contacts, Heaney was eventually offered a contract with Faber & Faber, who published his first volume of poems, *Death of a Naturalist*, in 1966, and who have remained his primary publishers ever since.

The poem which opens *Death of a Naturalist* is 'Digging'. It not only appears on the opening page of this volume, but also takes its place as the first poem in Heaney's *Selected Poems* (1980), his *New Selected Poems* (1990) and in *Opened Ground: Poems 1966–1996* (1998). Heaney indicates his sense of the poem's significance when he writes in *Preoccupations* that:

> 'Digging', in fact, was the name of the first poem I wrote where I thought my feelings had got into words, or to put it more accurately, where I thought my *feel* had got into words. ... I wrote it in the summer of 1964, almost two years after I had begun to 'dabble in verses'. This was the first place where I felt I had done more than make an arrangement of words: I felt that I had let down a shaft into real life. (P. 41)

8

As Heaney indicates here, he views 'Digging' as marking something like a point of departure for his career as a poet. We might say that this is true not only in terms of the poem's formal achievement in translating, as Heaney puts it, 'feeling into words', but also in the sense that 'Digging' registers, in small compass, many of the themes and concerns that would dominate his early poetry, in addition to providing an early glimpse of certain other issues that would surface as important elements later in his writing.

The language of 'Digging' introduces us to what will become, for much of his career, Heaney's dominant register. We can hear this verbal style at play in the next to last stanza of the poem, where Heaney writes:

> The cold smell of potato mould, the squelch and slap
> Of soggy peat, the curt cuts of an edge
> Through living roots awaken in my head.
>
> (DN 2)

Heaney deploys several verbal effects here to forge an evocative image of his subject. We find alliteration in 'the squelch and slap | Of soggy peat' and 'curt cuts'; assonance, a run of similar vowel sounds, in 'The cold smell of potato mould'; and onomatopoeia in 'squelch' and 'slap', which echo the sounds they describe. This kind of precise wielding of language to evoke a strong sense of the sight and sound of the world being described is entirely characteristic of Heaney's poetry and indicates the early influence on Heaney of the Victorian poet Gerard Manley Hopkins and also of Heaney's near contemporary, the English poet, Ted Hughes.[2] A similar set of effects is at play throughout *Death of a Naturalist*. Take, for instance, the following lines from the title poem of the collection:

> Bubbles gargled delicately, bluebottles
> Wove a strong gauze of sound around the smell.
>
> (DN 3)

and

> their loose necks pulsed like sails. Some hopped:
> The slap and plop were obscene threats. Some sat
> Poised like mud grenades, their blunt heads farting.
>
> (DN 4)

9

As Neil Corcoran has observed of this poem, 'the sheer noise Heaney manages to make out of English vowels here is remarkable – a dissonant cacophony that forces the mouth to work overtime if the reader speaks the lines aloud'.[3] Language is thus deployed here with enormous precision in order to evoke a detailed image of a very specific world, with Heaney taking pleasure in what he calls 'the rustle of language itself'.[4]

Where, verbally, we can trace the influence of Hopkins and Hughes in this early work, thematically we can register the influence that fellow Irish poet Patrick Kavanagh has had on Heaney's career. In an article on Kavanagh's poetry entitled 'The Placeless Heaven', included in *The Government of the Tongue*, Heaney writes of his excitement at first encountering Kavanagh's work:

> When I found 'Spraying the Potatoes' in the old *Oxford Book of Irish Verse*, I was excited to find details of a life which I knew intimately – but which I had always considered to be below or beyond books – being presented in a book. The barrels of blue potato spray which had stood in my own childhood like holidays of pure colour in an otherwise grey field-life – there they were, standing their ground in print. (*GT* 7)

Just as Kavanagh took as his subject matter his local native world of rural Monaghan, so Heaney in his turn renders in his poetry images of the life and landscape of the farming community where he grew up. Thus 'Digging' memorializes the cycles of manual labour on his family's farm – digging up potatoes and cutting turf on the bog. The titles of other poems in his first two collections point to a similar engagement with local issues and concerns. In *Death of a Naturalist* we find 'The Barn', 'Blackberry-Picking', 'Dawn Shoot', 'At a Potato Digging', 'Cow in Calf', and 'In Small Townlands', and in *Door into the Dark* we find 'The Forge', 'Thatcher', 'Rite of Spring', and 'Whinlands'. In a poem such as 'Churning Day' from *Death of a Naturalist* we can see Heaney's meticulous attention to detail as he attempts to recreate an exact image of the traditional local practices of butter-making:

> Out came the four crocks, spilled their heavy lip
> of cream, their white insides, into the sterile churn,
> The staff, like a great whisky muddler fashioned
> in deal wood, was plunged in, the lid fitted.
> My mother took first turn, set up rhythms

that slugged and thumped for hours. Arms ached.
Hands blistered. Cheeks and clothes were spattered
with flabby milk.
          Where finally gold flecks
began to dance. They poured hot water then,
sterilized a birchwood-bowl
and little corrugated butter-spades.

(*DN* 9)

We notice the painstaking accumulation of details here – the specificity of 'The staff . . . fashioned | in deal wood', the 'birchwood-bowl' and the 'corrugated butter-spades' – and, again, there is the evocative precision of much of the language used (the 'rhythms | that slugged and thumped for hours', for instance). Andrew Waterman has aptly observed of 'Churning Day' that 'reading the poem leaves one feeling that one has made the butter oneself'.[5]

These poems are, however, more than simply evocative descriptions. In common with Kavanagh, in memorializing the world of the familial and the local, Heaney is also attempting to work through the nature of his relationship to that world. In a revealing comment in 'The Placeless Heaven', Heaney observes that 'Kavanagh's genius had achieved singlehandedly what I and my grammar-schooled, arts-degreed generation were badly in need of – a poetry which linked the small farm life which produced us with the slim-volume world we were now supposed to be fit for. He brought us back to where we came from' (*GT* 9). Heaney thus sees Kavanagh as offering a link between the world of poetry and the local world of 'small farm life'. His comment indicates a certain alienation from this latter world which has resulted from his generation's having become 'grammar-schooled' and 'arts-degreed'. What Heaney is pointing to here is the fact that his generation was the first to benefit from the UK's 1947 Education Act, which significantly broadened access to secondary and university education, making it easier for students from less prosperous backgrounds to remain within the educational system for much longer than would tradition-ally have been the case. While access to education broadened the horizons of such students, it also served in some measure to alienate them from their communities and families, which, like

11

the Heaneys, in very many cases did not have a tradition of participating in advanced-level education.

'Digging' is itself centrally concerned with this issue of alienation and the need somehow to negotiate the distance between origins and present circumstances. Recalling his writing of 'Digging', Heaney remembers, in *Preoccupations*, the comments of the adults on neighbouring farms as he made his way to and from school: 'invariably they ended up with an exhortation to keep studying because "learning's easy carried" and "the pen's lighter than the spade" ' (*P.* 42). In the poem, 'learning' and the privileges to which it provides access are what separates the speaker from his father. The speaker sits inside, looking out at his father working beneath his window. In this sense, we might say that the growing cultural distance between the two is marked by the physical distance of their relative positions inside and outside the house, high at the window, low on the ground. Similarly, the shift in the speaker's class position (from the difficult circumstances of small farm life to educated middle-class security) is registered in the privileged position occupied by the speaker, as he has the luxury of being able to sit by and observe his father labouring outside.

The speaker in the poem experiences his privilege as effecting a kind of disjunction, emblematized by his relationship to the act of digging. In the narrative of the poem, digging serves to establish a sense of historical continuity: the father's digging now, in the poem's present, shifts easily to his 'com[ing] up twenty years away | Stooping in rhythm through potato drills | Where he was digging' (*DN* 1). This past activity of the father is in turn linked to the work of prior generations, following the same course in life: 'By God, the old man could handle a spade. | Just like his old man.' In his youth, the speaker in the poem has had a relationship of sorts to this extended tradition. He recalls, twenty years ago, picking up the potatoes unearthed by his father's digging:

> He rooted out tall tops, buried the bright edge deep
> To scatter new potatoes that we picked,
> Loving their cool hardness in our hands.

The appreciation for the feel of the newly exposed potatoes indicates a sense of connectedness between the boy and his environment. In a similar vein, the speaker in the poem recalls

12

having 'carried . . . milk in a bottle | Corked sloppily with paper' to his grandfather as he worked cutting turf 'on Toner's bog'. In both these instances, while the child figure's role is in some senses peripheral to the main activity of digging, he is, none the less, connected with that activity and with the traditional continuities that it signals. By contrast, the adult speaker feels entirely *disconnected* from this world. As an adult, he should be expected to take his place in the labouring line of his father and grandfather ('Just like his old man', as it were), but, instead, he is forced to observe: 'I've no spade to follow men like them' (*DN* 2).

Appropriately enough, we might think, the poet's recourse in these circumstances is to metaphor, as he concludes his poem by offering an analogy between the pen and the spade:

> Between my finger and my thumb
> The squat pen rests.
> I'll dig with it.

What Heaney suggests here is that the work he undertakes as a poet can be a kind of 'labour' of the same order as the work which has, for generations, been undertaken by his forebears. In this sense, though the poet cannot take his place in the extended line of labouring generations, he can, nevertheless, preserve the continuities represented by that line by encompassing that world within his poetry. If he cannot literally dig, he can 'dig' metaphorically, unearthing the details of the life of his family and community and honouring them by preserving them in his verse.[6] Or, as Helen Vendler puts it, these early poems memorialize 'a life which the poet does not want to follow, could not follow, but none the less recognizes as forever a part of his inner landscape'.[7]

In *Preoccupations*, Heaney offers us a more explicit rendering of the analogy between poetry and rural labour when he notes that ' "Verse" comes from the Latin *versus* which could mean the turn that a ploughman made at the head of the field as he finished one furrow and faced back into another' (*P.* 65). Heaney turns this scholarly perception to practical effect in 'Follower' – another poem from *Death of a Naturalist* in which the poet contemplates his relationship with his father. Heaney describes his father in 'Follower' as

> An expert. He would set the wing
> And fit the bright steel-pointed sock.

The sod rolled over without breaking.
At the headrig, with a single pluck
Of reins, the sweating team turned round
And back into the land.

(*DN* 12)

Heaney effects an immediate consonance here between his own unfolding act of poetic composition and his father's work with the plough. Where, in *Preoccupations*, Heaney registers an equivalence between the end of the ploughed furrow and the end of the poetic line, here the two physically mirror each other in the neat enjambment (that is, the 'turn over' from one poetic line into the next) of 'the sweating team turned round | And back into the land', where the turn of the verse itself matches exactly the turning of the horses it describes. Elsewhere in the poem, Heaney contrives similar effects, as in the case of the endstopped 'The sod rolled over without breaking.' – a line composed of a single sentence which, just like the unbroken turned sod it describes, maintains its own integrity (rather than, for instance, running on into the next line, as in the case of 'the sweating team turned round | And back . . .'). Again, the 'single pluck | | Of reins' occurs across a stanza break, reflecting the momentary drag and stay which pulls the horses round.

Viewed in this light, 'Follower' might appear to be a perfect formal enactment of the pledge which Heaney offers at the end of 'Digging': 'Between my finger and my thumb | The squat pen rests. | I'll dig with it.' Synthesizing metaphor and practice, he turns his pen here into a ploughshare; he effects a consonance between his poetic labour and the labour of his family and community and, in the process, he memorializes that labour in verse. As the poem draws to a close, however, we discover an unexpected note of disjunction emerging, as Heaney writes:

I wanted to grow up and plough,
To close one eye, stiffen my arm.
All I ever did was follow
In his broad shadow round the farm.

I was a nuisance, tripping, falling,
Yapping always. But today
It is my father who keeps stumbling
Behind me, and will not go away.

14

Despite the confident closure and paradigm of continuity established in 'Digging' and formally enacted throughout the early stanzas of 'Follower', then, the same conflicts which we found initially troubling the poet in 'Digging' endure here. In particular, we note the re-emergence of a generational conflict as the speaker is unable to establish an adequate relationship with his father. He finds their roles reversed, as he feels the weight of his father metaphorically dragging along behind him, just as he himself had literally dragged along behind his father when he was a child. The speaker is thus positioned in the poem between a sense of himself as a child, dependent on his father, and a mature sense of himself, struggling to establish his independence from his father and from his family generally.

A great many poems in *Death of a Naturalist* concern themselves with such moments of transition from childhood to maturity and, more particularly, with the cost incurred in acquiring the knowledge that puts an end to childhood innocence.[8] 'Death of a Naturalist', 'The Barn', 'An Advancement of Learning', 'Blackberry Picking', and 'Dawn Shoot' are just some of the poems that take up this theme. In 'The Barn' something menacing lurks within the dark confines of a farm building – a threat which the fearful speaker in the poem is unwilling and unable to encounter: 'I lay face-down to shun the fear above. | The two-lugged sacks moved in like great blind rats' (*DN* 5). In 'An Advancement of Learning', the poem which immediately follows 'The Barn' in *Death of a Naturalist*, the speaker *does* confront his fear, symbolized once again as a rat, this time encountered on a riverbank:

> The tapered tail that followed him,
> The raindrop eye, the old snout:
> One by one I took all in.
> He trained on me. I stared him out
>
> Forgetting how I used to panic
> When his grey brothers scraped and fed
> Behind the hen-coup in our yard,
> On ceiling boards above my bed.
>
> (*DN* 7)

In confronting his fear on this occasion, the speaker achieves a victory – the rat is forced into retreat and the speaker, still

15

holding his ground, 'stare[s] a minute after him'. The fruits of his victory are emblematically marked in the closing line of the poem, in which Heaney observes: 'Then I walked on and crossed the bridge'. This crossing of the bridge is clearly indicative of the successful negotiation of a certain 'rite of passage'. Having confronted his fear and triumphed, the speaker is free to move on to another stage in his journey.

'An Advancement of Learning' has a certain jubilant, jocular tone to it, as the speaker easily wins his battle of wills and emerges triumphant from his mock-heroic struggle with his emblematic adversary. 'Death of a Naturalist', by contrast, presents a much more conflicted and troubled picture. The first half of the poem produces an idyllic sense of an early springtime childhood, enjoyed within a beneficent natural order. The closing lines of this first section, however, signal an impending change, as they register a shift from the upbeat, positive 'yellow in the sun' to the dark and ominous 'brown | In rain' (DN 3) – an effect all the more marked by the fact that 'In rain' is set as a single line. In the second section of the poem, the frogspawn that has been gathered in section one comes to maturity and the natural world the speaker had enjoyed is overrun by adult frogs, which repulse him: 'I sickened, turned, and ran' (DN 4). As the narrative of the maturing of the frogspawn indicates, one of the fears registered in the poem is a fear of maturity itself – especially of sexual maturity. A strong thread of sexual imagery runs through the second section of the poem, as the frogs thicken the air with a 'bass chorus', sit 'cocked on sods', making 'obscene threats', 'their blunt heads farting'. As Michael Parker has observed, by the end of the poem 'innocent delight at the "warm thick slobber" has been replaced by disgust at his body's "spawn" '.[9] The narrative of the poem resists both maturity itself and an emerging sexual sense of self.

If 'Death of a Naturalist' is a poem about the difficult transition from childhood to adolescence, and the simultaneous fascination and repulsion of sexual awakenings, many of the later poems in Heaney's first collection concern themselves with a more fully adult transition – from the independence of single life to the responsibilities of marriage. Heaney's turning to such subject matter is not too surprising, given that just a year before Death of a Naturalist was published he had married Marie

Devlin, a fellow Northern Irish schoolteacher. As in the earlier poems in the collection, many of the marriage pieces concern themselves with the crossing of a threshold from one state of life to another. The uncertainties of the threshold state itself – where one lingers between one positioning and the next – are nicely caught in a poem such as 'Honeymoon Flight'. Here the airborne transition between two points of a journey reflects the moment of suspension between an old life left behind and a new life in prospect:

> And launched right off the earth by force of fire,
> We hang, miraculous, above the water,
> Dependent on the invisible air
> To keep us airborne and to bring us further.

> (DN 36)

The stanza holds together the four traditional elements of earth, fire, water, and air, in an act of balance mirroring that achieved by the aircraft itself in flight. As the poem draws to a close, the horizon of a new life opens up. The poem ends: 'Air-pockets jolt our fears and down we go. | Travellers, at this point, can only trust.' At a literal level, of course, the 'trust' in question here is being placed in the pilot of the aircraft, to bring it in safely to land, but it also indicates the trust that must be placed in the married state itself, to fulfill the lives of the individual partners.

The most striking of the marriage poems included in *Death of a Naturalist* is a short piece entitled 'Lovers on Aran'. Heaney has often been (justly) criticized for deploying male/female binaries in his poems in a manner which presents the female as passive, yielding, accepting – the powerless recipient of an active, dominating, dynamic male. As Patricia Coughlan has observed, frequently in his poems Heaney 'constructs an unequivocally dominant masculine figure, who explores, describes, brings to pleasure and compassionates a passive feminine one'.[10] In 'Lovers on Aran', however, in a set of interesting inversions and reversals, Heaney actually presents an interrogation of these very gender stereotypes. He begins with an image of the waves swarming in 'To possess Aran' (DN 34). But the act of possession signalled is an odd one, as the waves come in to take their possession 'from the Americas'. The 'geography' of this image is logical enough – the Atlantic waves wash in eastward onto

17

the shores of the Aran islands, which lie off the west coast of Ireland. But, in addition to the geography, there is also a historical reference at play here. The thrust of colonial possession has always been westward, not eastward. Historically (especially in the sixteenth and early seventeenth centuries), Ireland frequently served as a staging point for colonizing expeditions setting out to possess the Americas. Here, in an inversion of historical precedent, the direction of possession is reversed – the waves flow from the New World to possess a corner of the Old. We might also notice that, whereas Heaney most typically associates water – fluid, yielding, formless – with the passive female (see, for instance, 'Undine' and 'Rite of Spring' in *Door into the Dark*), here the water is initially given a certain masculine value, being presented as, essentially, 'penetrating' the land. But these alignments are quickly complicated. Having detailed the sea's act of possession, Heaney asks:

> Or did Aran rush
> To throw wide arms of rock around a tide
> That yielded with an ebb, with a soft crash?

This cancels the active, aggressive image of irruption, as the inflow of the waters may constitute as much an act of enfolding by the land as of penetration by the sea. Having thus rendered the alignments and significances of his imagery ambiguous, Heaney goes on to ask: 'Did sea define the land or land the sea?' – an unanswerable question which presents the lovers as united in a relationship of mutuality and equality. In the broader sweep of the poem, the question leaves fruitfully open issues of definition and identity, in a way that will not be typical of much of Heaney's other poetry in which the issue of gender is prominently featured.

'Lovers on Aran' is one of two poems set on the islands in *Death of a Naturalist*, the other being one of the last poems in the collection, entitled 'Synge on Aran'. This latter poem is concerned with the Irish playwright, John Millington Synge, who, between 1898 and 1902, spent long periods on the islands. Synge's project as a dramatist was to provide an accurate picture of rural life in Ireland and to find a way of reproducing in English some of the rhythms, textures, and nuances of the Irish language. Heaney conceives of him with

> a hard pen
> scraping in his head;
> the nib filed on a salt wind
> and dipped in the keening sea.
>
> (*DN* 39)

Just as Heaney imagines himself in 'Digging' as adapting his own pen to the unearthing task of the spade, so here he imagines Synge as fashioning *his* pen upon the environment he wishes to describe – sharpening his nib on the abrasive wind, the mournful sea his ink.

This image of Synge at the end of *Death of a Naturalist* takes us back to Heaney's other important literary precursor, Patrick Kavanagh. As it happens, Kavanagh had little time for Synge. He felt that Synge and his privileged middle-class Protestant literary colleagues lacked, as outside observers, any true connection with the realities of country life and simply romanticized the figure of the peasant and grossly misrepresented life as it was actually lived in rural Ireland (a point most forcibly made in Kavanagh's poetry in *The Great Hunger*). For all that, there is much that unites Kavanagh, Synge, and Heaney as writers from three different generations seeking to accomplish certain things within their work. Both Synge and Kavanagh pledge a certain fidelity to the precise details of the purely local, believing that, if one is faithful to such local concerns, they will of themselves open outwards to something greater, something more universal in its significance. Kavanagh draws a distinction between 'provincialism', on the one hand, and 'parochialism', on the other. 'A provincial', he writes, 'is always trying to live by other people's loves, but a parochial is self-sufficient.' Kavanagh's clearest statement of faith in the parochial in his poetry is delivered in his well-known poem, 'Epic'. In this poem, Kavanagh remembers a particular dispute in his native area which inflamed local passions intensely. Recollecting that the events took place on the eve of the Second World War, he yields to a moment of self-doubt, wondering whether these local incidents can be said to be in any way significant in the face of such great upheaval. As the poem draws to a close, however, this doubt is banished and his faith in the local is reaffimed:

> That was the year of the Munich bother. Which
> Was more important? I inclined

19

To lose my faith in Ballyrush and Gortin
Till Homer's ghost came whispering to my mind.
He said: I made the Iliad from such
A local row. Gods make their own importance.[11]

The great epic of the *Iliad*, the story of the Trojan War, is here
reduced to its origins as 'a local row' – a petty dispute, we might
say, between the Greek Menelaus and the Trojan Paris over
which of them should have Menelaus' wife, Helen. It is the very
act of poetic memorialization itself, Kavanagh suggests (through
Homer), that lends the local story its significance, that creates
the epic, drawing the universal from the particular.

We have already noted the significance of Kavanagh's poetic
practice to Heaney earlier in this chapter when we discussed
Heaney's attempt to encompass his domestic world within his
poetry and thereby to effect a sense of continuity with his community and to work through the nature of his relationship to
his origins. Kavanagh's broader perspective on the nature and
function of poetry is also of great relevance to Heaney's work,
especially as he begins both to develop further and to move
beyond the themes which we have seen him explore in *Death of
a Naturalist*. In an early comment on Kavanagh, in an article published in the *Listener*, Heaney observed that 'Kavanagh enhances
our view of the world, and makes us feel that any task, in
any place, is an important act, in an important place',[12] and, in
Heaney's second and third collections, *Door into the Dark* and
Wintering Out, we find several poems in which, like Kavanagh,
he focuses upon the minute particularities of the local in order
to expose within them traces of a greater world. 'The Forge' from
Door into the Dark is a case in point. It opens with the line 'All
I know is a door into the dark' (*DD* 7) which, in addition to
giving the collection its title, also resonates with the very last
line of *Death of a Naturalist*, where, in 'Personal Helicon', Heaney
proclaims that he writes poetry in order 'to set the darkness
echoing' (*DN* 44). The connection between the two poems is
significant, as Heaney often ends one collection of his work
with a piece which, in effect, will serve as a sort of 'manifesto'
for the collection to follow.

The opening line of 'The Forge' seems to indicate that what
Heaney's poetic art gives him is a point of penetration into
the heart of a world which is beyond the everyday, but which

proves to be somehow simultaneously central to it. By contrast with 'The Barn', where the speaker in the poem is unwilling to enter into the darkness, afraid of what he might find there, the speaker in 'The Forge' seeks to go into the darkness, to see what lies beyond, or *within*, the outside world. What he finds is indeed something that 'sets the darkness echoing' – the hammer-blows of the blacksmith working a new horseshoe upon his anvil, set at the centre of the forge. Heaney brings his usual eye for detail to bear on the blacksmith in the poem, as, in a few short but evocatively accurate strokes, he provides us with a pen picture of him: 'leather-aproned, hairs in his nose, | He leans out on the jamb . . . Then grunts and goes in.' The ordinariness of this picture comes as something of a surprise and contrasts with the exotic creatures Heaney's earlier poetic speaker imagined inhabited the darkness of 'The Barn' – 'bright eyes' staring 'From piles of grain in corners, fierce, unblinking', 'bats . . . on the wing', 'two-lugged sacks . . . like great blind rats'. The smith's peripheral and oddly anachronistic status is registered in the poem when Heaney sketches an image of him, in his momentary rest from his work, recalling 'a clatter | Of hoofs where traffic is flashing in rows'. The horse having been superseded by the car, the smith is, in this context, a representative of a dying trade. But even as he is presented as ordinary, peripheral, outdated in the poem, the smith is also centralized, just as his anvil is centred within the forge itself. He is consciously imagined within the poem as a figure for the poet-as-maker, a figure not unlike that of another 'blacksmith' – the Hephaestus of the Homeric epics who, though crippled and cuckolded, is capable of producing work of great beauty and intricacy and who, crucially, is able to encompass an entire universe on the decorative surface of a single shield, when asked by Thetis to forge armour for her son Achilles:

> Five welded layers
> composed the body of the shield. The maker
> used all his art adorning this expanse.
> He pictured on it earth, heaven, and sea,
> unwearied sun, moon waxing, all the stars
> that heaven bears for garland . . . [13]

Heaney's smith, as he is like Homer's Hephaestus, is also, we might say, like Kavanagh's Homer, in that he is the one who

21

forges enduring significance from base material, beating 'real iron out', expending 'himself in shape and music', and creating a whole world within small compass.

The poem which follows 'The Forge' in *Door into the Dark* – 'Thatcher' – charts a very similar sort of trajectory. Again the poem concerns a practitioner of a dying trade – the job of the thatcher is to tend to the traditional roofwork of cottages that are covered in straw, or 'thatch', an increasing rarity as more and more rural homes are modernized. The tools, materials, and techniques of this skilled craftsman are meticulously described in the poem. The thatcher turns up

> Unexpectedly, his bicycle slung
> With a light ladder and a bag of knives.
> He eyed the old rigging, poked at the eaves,
>
> Opened and handled sheaves of lashed wheat-straw.
> Next, the bundled rods: hazel and willow
> Were flicked for weight, twisted in case they'd snap.
>
> (*DD* 8)

Like the blacksmith, the thatcher is a figure for the creative intelligence who, though peripheral and rather outmoded, is nevertheless capable of producing from the ordinary ('straw . . . rods . . . a white-pronged staple . . . sods') something extraordinary, something wondrous:

> Couchant for days on sods above the rafters,
> He shaved and flushed the butts, stitched all together
> Into a sloped honeycomb, a stubble patch,
> And left them gaping at his Midas touch.

Robert Welch has noted the connection between Heaney's 'Thatcher' and the sixteenth-century English poet Sir Philip Sidney's theoretical treatise *A Defence of Poetry*, in which Sidney, contrasting the works of art and of nature, comments that, where nature's 'world is brazen [i.e. made of brass], the poets only deliver a golden' world.[14] Both Sidney, then, and Heaney (through the figure of the thatcher with his 'Midas' touch) posit a transformative, alchemical power for poetry: the power to take the ready material of the everyday and to fashion it into something astounding. In a sense we might say that 'The Forge' and 'Thatcher' represent Heaney's own 'Defence of Poetry', his own version of Kavanagh's 'Epic', in which he affirms the power of poetry to transform, to find in the everyday and the particular something greater, something more significant.

If 'The Forge' and 'Thatcher' are, then, in some sense 'theoretical' poems, signalling a kind of poetic manifesto, in other poems in *Door into the Dark* and *Wintering Out* we find that theory put into practice. This is particularly true of the group of 'place-name' poems which Heaney includes in the second of these collections – 'Anahorish', 'Toome', and 'Broagh' (whose very titles are taken from place-names) and also 'Gifts of Rain' and 'A New Song'. In these poems, Heaney unites a theory of poetry with a theory of language itself. On the one hand, following Kavanagh, Heaney believes that poetry can find something greater than the particular in the local; on the other, from another Irish poetic source – the ancient native Irish poetic tradition of *dinnseanchas* – he derives a sense that the language of local naming bears within itself a kind of compressed narrative of local history. Just as Kavanagh believes that an engagement with the particularities of the local can open outwards to a greater world, so the *dinnseanchas* tradition suggests that a kind of etymological investigation of local naming can open up the greater history of the named place. Thus, as Henry Hart indicates, 'Etymology, in Heaney's hands, lays bare the poetic fossil within the linguistic core'.[15]

In *Preoccupations* Heaney writes of 'the cultural depth-charges latent in certain words and rhythms':

> that binding secret between words in poetry that delights not just the ear but the whole backward and abysm of mind and body ... the energies beating in and between words that the poet brings into half-deliberate play ... the relationship between the word as pure vocable, as articulate noise, and the word as etymological occurrence, as symptom of human history, memory and attachments. (P. 150)

This captures the essence of Heaney's view of the *dinnseanchas* tradition: his belief that language itself – and, specifically, the language of proper naming – carries within itself a kind of native history, an etymologically etched memory 'rapidly seiz[ing] a world from a word', as Neil Corcoran puts it.[16] We can see this notion at play in 'Anahorish', the first of the place-name poems from *Wintering Out*. The name 'Anahorish' is an anglicized conflation of the native Irish *anach fhíor uisce* and Heaney begins

23

his poem with a translation of the Irish, as he writes: 'My "place of clear water" ' (WO 6).[17] From this unveiling of the literal meaning of 'Anahorish', Heaney, in a move that might remind us of Kavanagh, goes on to posit the place of his origins as a kind of primally original place, as it becomes

> the first hill in the world
> where springs washed into
> the shiny grass
>
> and darkened cobbles
> in the bed of the lane.

From here, Heaney returns to the name itself, atomizing it, considering its constituent parts: 'Anahorish, soft gradient | of consonant, vowel-meadow'. Heaney believes that he finds here, in the phonetic elements of the word itself, an image of the very landscape to which the name is attached, as consonant and vowel combine to reflect the rise and fall of the land.

In the final two stanzas, the poem opens up, moving from the specificities of geography to the residues of history. Faintly perceived human figures enter the landscape which the first two stanzas have established. At first they seem virtually an effect of the name itself, as Heaney writes

> *Anahorish*, soft gradient
> of consonant, vowel-meadow,
>
> after-image of lamps
> swung through the yards
> on winter evenings.

The place-name itself triggers a residual image not of the inhabitants of the place but of the lights which they carry. In the closing lines of the poem the inhabitants themselves finally emerge into the light, but even now they are seen obscurely, through a mist:

> With pails and barrows
>
> those mound-dwellers
> go waist-deep in mist
> to break the light ice
> at wells and dunghills.

What Heaney has offered us in the poem, then, is a process whereby, through scrutinizing the particularities of a proper name, we are able to understand its meaning, its connection to

24

its place of application, and its position of centrality. Beyond the geography of this linguistically demarcated place, we are able to catch a glimpse of its human history. Through the rough glass of the name we can see an image of the original, ancient inhabitants of the place.

Heaney angles for analogous effects in the other place-name poems included in *Wintering Out*. In 'Gifts of Rain', the name of the local river, Moyola, is imagined as offering a similar self-image as that perceived in 'Anahorish': 'The tawny gutteral water I spells itself: Moyola I is its own score and consort' (*WO* 15). The name offers a kind of internal harmony, redolent of local affairs: 'reed music, an old chanter I I breathing its mists through vowels and history.' Some of the specificities of the 'history' evoked here begin to emerge in 'Toome', 'A New Song', and 'Broagh'. In 'Toome' we find Heaney exploring a name which has a lightly explosive quality as it is spoken: 'My mouth holds round I the soft blast-ings, I *Toome, Toome*' (*WO* 16). As Heaney digs down through its history, pushing 'into a souterrain I prospecting', he unearths the remnants of history. In among the bric-à-brac of forgotten daily lives – the 'loam, flints', 'fragmented ware', and 'fish-bones' – he finds 'musket-balls', a token of the country's explosive and conflictual past.

The contours of that past and Heaney's sense of how the narrative of history is intertwined with language itself emerge in 'A New Song'. In this poem, the speaker encounters a native of Derrygarve and the place-name spurs the poet to his usual local analysis. As in the case of 'Anahorish', 'Derrygarve' calls up through Heaney's *dinnseanchas* machinery potent images of local geography. The poem turns, however, around the fulcrum of its middle stanza, where Heaney writes:

> And Derrygarve, I thought, was just,
> Vanished music, twilit water,
> A smooth libation of the past
> Poured by this chance vestal daughter.
>
> (*WO* 23)

Where in 'Anahorish' the trajectory of the poem is to open out towards a vision of an ancient community which, while faintly perceived, is nevertheless imagined as living in the flow of daily life ('break[ing] the light ice I at wells and dunghills'), here, in

25

'A New Song', we register an image of a life that is imagined as irretrievably past. In contrast with 'Gifts of Rain', where the Moyola is 'A swollen river' echoing an active and regenerative 'mating call of sound', the same river here presents a 'twilit water' and the general feeling of the stanza is of an irreversible dwindling and fading – from twilight towards the darkness of endless night, as it were. Reading the poem allegorically, we can see it as registering, up to this point, a lament for a native culture that has been lost as a result of Ireland's colonial history. Native Irish civilization is, in this regard, little more than a 'vanished music'. As the poem moves into its final two stanzas, however, a significant shift occurs:

> But now our river tongues must rise
> From licking deep in native haunts
> To flood, with vowelling embrace,
> Demesnes staked out in consonants.
>
> And Castledawson we'll enlist
> And Upperlands, each planted bawn –
> Like bleaching-greens resumed by grass –
> A vocable, as rath and bullaun.

What Heaney presents here is, in fact, a narrative of *decolonization*. The native language returns to supplant the language that banished it – overrunning the imperial 'demesnes' and 'consonants' (Heaney has written in *Preoccupations* that he thinks 'of the personal and Irish pieties as vowels, and the literary awarenesses nourished on English as consonants', (*P.* 37)) and displacing the alien imposed names of 'Castledawson' and 'Upperlands'. Heaney's image for this displacement is the repossession of the 'bleaching-greens' (emblematic of the linen industry introduced into the north of Ireland by Protestant colonists) by the native grass (symbolic of the native Irish pastoral farming tradition) – a taking back of the land from the colonist. The final word in the poem is literally given to the native, as Heaney invokes the Irish 'rath' (hill-fort) and 'bullaun' (hollowed stone mortar).[18]

If 'A New Song' is in some measure charged with the energy of nationalist, anti-colonialist aspiration, Heaney offers us a rather different aspiration in 'Broagh'. Neil Corcoran has observed of 'Broagh' that it 'has a significance in Heaney's work altogether disproportionate to its length',[19] and it is certainly true that this short poem is immensely rich and resonant. In the second and third stanzas of the poem Heaney offers his usual reading of geography into the place-name ('the shower I gathering in your heelmark I was the black *O* I I in *Broagh*' (*WO* 17)). In the first stanza, however, we get something rather different from the standard *dinnseanchas* performance:

> Riverba[n]k,[20] the long rigs
> ending in broad docken
> and a canopied pad
> down to the ford.

Heaney is being immensely precise in his choice of language here. The opening word of the poem offers a translation of 'broagh' itself, which is an anglicized version of the Irish *bruach*, meaning 'riverbank'. Heaney ends this first line, however, with the word 'rigs' – meaning 'furrows' – a word brought to the north of Ireland by seventeenth-century Scots colonists. Elsewhere in this same stanza Heaney offers us the dialect words 'docken' and 'pad', both of which, again, have strong connections with Scots. What Heaney creates in this first stanza then, is a kind of common language community that unites colonizer and native.

This union is thrown into relief in the closing stanza of the poem, where Heaney comments on the pronunciation of *broagh*, noting 'that last I *gh* the strangers found I difficult to manage'. The harsh-sounding final phoneme of 'Broagh' indicates a sound that has been largely lost within the English language, but which is still available to native and colonizer alike in the language community of the north of Ireland. Linguistically, then, the correct pronunciation of 'Broagh' serves simultaneously to unite the divided communities of the North and to set them apart from the alien community of the English, divided from them by sea and sound, as it were. What Heaney seems to be offering is an image of the union of the two traditions of the North – an internal union which detaches the territory from its union with England.

John Kerrigan offers a contrasting interpretation of what Heaney is attempting in 'Broagh'. While granting the ethnic and ethical complexity of Heaney's manoeuvrings, he nevertheless feels that they ultimately serve an attempt to retrieve an essential Irish identity, rather than adequately engaging with the complexities of identity *per se*:

27

although the reader of, say 'the black O // in *Broagh*' does not need to know that *bruach* ('riverbank') has no 'o' in Gaelic, the scrambling of the place name by Anglicization, and the tangential accessibility of 'that last / *gh* the strangers found / difficult to manage' to locals of Scottish stock, does make the title-word of 'Broagh' a site of some historical and philological complexity. But Heaney feels no imaginative urge or responsibility to make this explicit in the poem, not just because it would disrupt his lyric textures if he engaged in a dictionary-thumbing . . . but because his poetic instincts are inseparable at this stage from a politics which wants to find, under the layers of linguistic colonialism, a more authentic in-placeness in Gaelic than in an hybrid vocable.[21]

Kerrigan's astute reservations notwithstanding, it is clear that in these poems Heaney is attempting to engage with the fraught political and historical situation in Ireland – albeit in a rather oblique fashion.[22] When *Wintering Out* appeared in 1972, the situation in Northern Ireland had reached a point of crisis. In the next chapter we will examine Heaney's response to that crisis in greater detail.

2

'Where the fault is opening': Politics and Mythology

Wintering Out opens with a poem of dedication to David Hammond and the Northern Irish poet Michael Longley:

> This morning from a dewy motorway
> I saw the new camp for the internees:
> a bomb had left a crater of fresh clay
> in the roadside, and over in the trees
>
> machine-gun posts defined a real stockade.
> There was that white mist you get on a low ground
> and it was déjà-vu, some film made
> of Stalag 17, a bad dream with no sound.
>
> Is there life before death? That's chalked up
> on a wall downtown. Competence with pain,
> coherent miseries, a bite and sup,
> we hug our little destiny again.
>
> (*WO*, p. v)

As a point of entry into Heaney's third collection of poems, this piece (later incorporated into 'Whatever You Say Say Nothing' in *North*) offers us a glimpse of a very different world from the one we are introduced to on the opening page of *Death of a Naturalist*. Where 'Digging' presents us with a natural, rural world of 'flowerbeds', 'potato drills', 'new potatoes', 'good turf', and 'living roots' (*DN* 1, 2), Heaney's poem for Hammond and Longley brings us face to face with a harsh new set of realities. Northern Ireland had changed quite dramatically between 1966, when *Death of a Naturalist* was published, and 1972, when

29

Wintering Out appeared, and many of these changes are registered here in this poem of dedication.

As the 1960s ended, the Northern Irish state lurched towards crisis. With the failure of the Civil Rights movement, militant republicanism (and militant unionism) revived and the province grew accustomed both to the sounds and to the consequences of bombings and shootings. As Heaney drives along the motorway (in itself something of an incongrous intrusion of the modern world into his typical poetic *mise-en-scène* – at least up to this point in his career), he sees the crater which a bomb has scarred into the landscape. As a result of the deepening crisis, the British Army were now deployed in the North and they, too, intrude into the scene, with their 'machine-gun posts defin[ing] a real stockade'. In August of the previous year the government had introduced internment without trial, and hundreds of people (almost all of them Catholics) had been rounded up and detained in camps like the one that Heaney sees from the motorway. The whole scene has, for the poet, an air of unreality about it. Hardly able to believe that the situation can have come to this, he likens what confronts him to a scene from a bad war movie.

For all the shock of encountering this scene, however, the final stanza of the poem registers less surprise at new developments than resignation in the face of the recognizably familiar. The slogan chalked up on a Belfast wall – 'Is there life before death?' – indicates a certain grim humour, the kind of weary cynicism that comes from bitter familiarity with suffering. In the closing lines of the poem, an entire community settles down to the desperate mundanity of the reopened wounds of old conflict.

Though Heaney finds himself brought into direct confrontation with the latest manifestation of this conflict as he opens *Wintering Out*, in fact, if we look back through both *Door into the Dark* and *Death of a Naturalist*, we can trace the pulse of that conflict even in his earliest work. It is no coincidence, we might feel, that, even in 'Digging', Heaney's pen is imagined first as a gun before it becomes a spade ('Between my finger and my thumb I The squat pen rests; snug as a gun' (*DN* 1)). Such images are surprisingly insistent throughout his early poems. In 'Churning Day', for instance, 'the four crocks' stand in the small pantry like 'large pottery bombs' (*DN* 9); in 'Trout', the fish 'Hangs, a fat gun-barrel', 'his muzzle gets bull's eye', his food is 'torpedoed', he 'darts like a tracer- I bullet', 'A volley of cold blood I I ramrodding the current' (*DN* 26); 'In Small Townlands' presents us with the following lines: 'The spectrum bursts, a bright grenade, I When he unlocks the safety catch I On morning dew, on cloud, on rain' (*DN* 41). What we discover here is an assimilation of the language of conflict (or, in some cases, we might say, the *intrusion* of the language of conflict) into the metaphoric register of the poems.

Elsewhere in the early poems Heaney addresses the issue of the conflict itself more directly. 'At a Potato Digging' and 'For the Commander of the *Eliza*' in *Death of a Naturalist*, and 'Requiem for the Croppies' from *Door into the Dark*, are all poems which take up aspects of the history of the conflict in Ireland. The first two poems concern themselves with the Great Famine (1845–51), when perhaps a million people died as a result of the failure of the potato crop in Ireland in several successive years (with about a further million emigrating from Ireland in the same period). Potatoes were the staple diet of the Irish peasantry. In 'At a Potato Digging' Heaney opens with a description of a contemporary farming scene: 'A mechanical digger wrecks the drill', churning up the potatoes, as a group of 'Labourers swarm in behind' (*DN* 18) to gather in the crop. In the third section of the poem, however, the scene shifts and we are presented with a stark image of the famine victims of the previous century:

> Live skulls, blind-eyed, balanced on
> wild higgledy skeletons,
> scoured the land in 'forty-five,
> wolfed the blighted root and died.
>
> · · · · ·
>
> Mouths tightened in, eyes died hard,
> faces chilled to a plucked bird.
> In a million wicker huts,
> beaks of famine snipped at guts.

> (*DN* 19)

As the section draws to a close, we are returned to the contemporary scene, but with the knowledge that, beneath the surface of this modern world, lies the unhealed wound of the famine experience: 'where potato diggers are, I you still smell the running sore' (*DN* 20).

31

In the immediately following poem in *Death of a Naturalist*, 'For the Commander of the *Eliza*', Heaney takes up the question of where political responsibility for the tragedy of the famine lies. Following the work of the historian Cecil Woodham-Smith, he implicitly rejects the view that the famine deaths are merely to be ascribed to natural causes, finding, instead, a certain culpability in the calculated inaction of the colonial authorities. The poem is dedicated to the captain of a coastguard boat who encounters six starving Irishmen adrift in a small rowboat. They beg him for food and he refuses, but later, haunted by the image of the 'Six wrecks of bone and pallid, tautened skin' (*DN* 21), he reports the incident to his Inspector General, who orders a better distribution of relief to famine victims in the area, and receives a reprimand from the government authorities in London for his trouble. The poem closes with the Captain's ironic rendering of London's response:

> Let natives prosper by their own exertions;
> Who could not swim might go ahead and sink.
> 'The Coast Guard with their zeal and activity
> Are too lavish' were the words, I think.
>
> (*DN* 22)

The lack of compassion and concern exhibited by the authorities in 'For the Commander of the *Eliza*' serves to symbolize the consequences of Ireland's colonial experience and the suffering which it occasioned. In 'Requiem for the Croppies' Heaney takes up the other side of the colonial equation – the history of Irish resistance to English domination. The poem was written in 1966, when the fiftieth anniversary of the 1916 uprising (which eventually led to independence for the larger portion of the island of Ireland) was being celebrated. 'Requiem' does not deal directly with the uprising, but rather harks back to another revolutionary moment – the 1798 'United Irishmen' rebellion, which was rigorously suppressed by the British. The 'United Irishmen' were a fragile coalition of radical protestants and militant catholics, whose doctrine was inspired in large measure by the French Revolution. Prominent among the leadership of the movement was the Protestant Theobald Wolfe Tone, who holds a central position within the pantheon of Irish republicanism.[1] As John Kerrigan notes in relation to 'Broagh', however, it is not the transcultural complexity and political multifacetedness of the United

Irishmen that hold Heaney's attention, but rather the fate of a single, largely catholic group who were killed during the uprising in the southeastern county of Wexford. In this incident a large group of 'croppies' (young fighters who cut their hair short in imitation of the peasants in the French Revolution) made a last-ditch stand against the British on Vinegar Hill in Wexford and were cut down, defeated by the superior technology of British weaponry: 'Terraced thousands died, shaking scythes at cannon' (*DD* 12). In closing the poem, however, Heaney offers an image of regeneration: 'They buried us without shroud or coffin I And in August the barley grew up out of the grave.' In *Preoccupations*, Heaney offers his own gloss on these lines:

> The poem was born of and ended with an image of resurrection based on the fact that some time after the rebels were buried in common graves, these graves began to sprout with young barley, growing up from barley corn which the 'croppies' had carried in their pockets to eat while on the march. The oblique implication was that the seeds of violent resistance sowed in the Year of Liberty [1798] had flowered in what Yeats called 'the right rose tree' of 1916. (*P.* 56)

What Heaney seeks to do, then, in 'Requiem for the Croppies' is to effect a sense of historical continuity between Irish acts of resistance across the centuries – from the uprising of 1798 to that of 1916. In another poem from *Death of a Naturalist*, 'Docker', he engages less with the historical sweep of the conflict as it has played itself out throughout the island than with the bigotry and barely contained sectarian violence of the Northern Ireland he has experienced in his own lifetime. The poem presents a portrait of a working-class Protestant engaged in Belfast's notoriously discriminatory shipbuilding industry. He fancies this figure as utterly unyielding, built of steel, just like the vessels he spends his life working on. His hatred of Catholics is registered in the second stanza of the poem:

> That fist would drop a hammer on a Catholic –
> Oh yes, that kind of thing could start again.
> The only Roman collar he tolerates
> Smiles all round his sleek pint of porter.

> (*DN* 28)

'Docker' is uncharacteristically explicit in its engagement with the situation in the North. Heaney himself has associated the poem with 'the slightly aggravated young Catholic male part' of his temperament which he says he suppressed elsewhere in his early poetry in favour of 'the private county Derry childhood part' of himself.[2] The poem is, however, strikingly prophetic, with its expectation that sectarian conflict could well be revived in the North.

Writing of the eventual outbreak of that anticipated revival of conflict in 1969 and of his response to it as a poet, Heaney observes in *Preoccupations* that

> From that moment the problems of poetry moved from being simply a matter of achieving the satisfactory verbal icon to being a search for images and symbols adequate to our predicament. . . . I felt it imperative to discover a field of force in which, without abandoning fidelity to the processes and experience of poetry . . . it would be possible to encompass the perspectives of a humane reason and at the same time to grant the religious intensity of the violence its deplorable authenticity and complexity. (*P*. 56–7)

In pursuing this 'search for images and symbols adequate to our predicament', Heaney found himself drawn to a book entitled *The Bog People*, written by P. V. Glob and published in an English translation in Northern Ireland's watershed year of 1969. As Heaney himself notes, the book 'was chiefly concerned with preserved bodies of men and women found in the bogs of Jutland, naked, strangled or with their throats cut, disposed under the peat since early Iron Age times' (*P*. 57). Heaney was attracted to the book because it both served to focus a number of his traditional interests, and also offered him a particular frame of reference and set of symbols which he could deploy in engaging with the present conflict and its antecedent history.

The attractions of an account of the preservative and historically retentive powers of bogland to the author of a poem such as 'Digging' should be obvious. In *Preoccupations*, indeed, Heaney imagines 'Digging' itself as having been 'dug up', rather than written, observing that he has 'come to realize that it was laid down in me years ago' (*P*. 42). In this sense, the poetic act is one of 'retrieval' – of recovering something that already exists – rather than of creating something entirely new from whole cloth. This notion of retrieving what has been preserved but occluded resonates with Heaney's sense of the tradition of *dinnseanchas*. In the place-name poems, we remember, Heaney sought to excavate the hidden histories which are compacted in a local name. Bogland, in fact, provides a perfect analogy for this sense of the relationship between locale and history, since bogland literally preserves material elements of a particular region's past, yielding them up when the land is excavated. As Heaney observes in *Preoccupations*, bog serves as 'the memory of the landscape, or as a landscape that remember[s] everything that happened in and to it' (*P*. 54). Heaney gives his clearest poetic expression to this idea in a poem entitled 'Kinship' from *North*, in which he characterizes bogland as

> Ruminant ground,
> digestion of mollusc
> and seed-pod,
> deep pollen-bin.
>
> Earth-pantry, bone vault,
> sun-bank, embalmer
> of votive goods
> and sabred fugitives.
>
> Insatiable bride.
> Sword-swallower,
> casket, midden,
> floe of history.
>
> (*N*. 34)

Bogland is presented here as an insatiable and consuming ground that indiscriminately swallows all that comes to it and preserves it intact, as a kind of treasure trove to be yielded up in time.

Heaney's first attempt at exploiting the poetic potential of the symbolism of bogland comes in a poem of that very name, which closes *Door into the Dark*. The positioning of the poem at the end of the collection is important, since, as in the case of *Death of a Naturalist*'s 'Personal Helicon', it serves to indicate a significant direction Heaney will pursue in his future work. The preservative power of the bog is graphically indicated in the third stanza of 'Bogland', where the massive frame of an Irish deer rises up out of the land:

> They've taken the skeleton
> Of the Great Irish Elk
> Out of the peat, set it up
> An astonishing crate full of air.
>
> (*DD* 41)

35

In contrast to the grandeur of this image, the next object to emerge from the bog in the poem is butter, an everyday domestic necessity, 'recovered salty and white'. Taken together, the elk and the butter signify the heterogeneity of the bog, its tendency to preserve everything, without selecting out a particular set of objects. In the closing stanzas of the poem we learn that the process of excavation is potentially endless. The layers of the bog lead to no final resting place, but simply reveal a bottomless centre:

> Our pioneers keep striking
> Inwards and downwards,
> Every layer they strip
> Seems camped on before.
> The bogholes might be Atlantic seepage.
> The wet centre is bottomless.
>
> (DD 41–2)

Heaney returns to the theme of preservation and the deep world to which it gives access in *Wintering Out*. He first takes up the issue in 'Bog Oak', a poem not about the bog itself, but about a piece of seasoned wood, retrieved from the bog and used as building material. The speaker in the poem remembers the beam as 'a cobwebbed, black | long-seasoned rib | | under the first thatch' (*WO* 4), indicating that it has served as a roof-beam in his own family home. In the manner of some of the place-name poems, the memory of this rafter calls up images of an entire native community – not just the speaker's own immediate family but, we sense, a gathering of his ancestors stretching back into a communal past. The poem offers us a kind of cinematic effect, as we move from the interior of the family dwelling to the door, where we are presented with a view through the 'mizzling rain' to 'the far end | of the cart track'. In the final two stanzas of the poem, we discover what is just about visible at the end of that track:

> Perhaps I just make out
> Edmund Spenser,
> dreaming sunlight,
> encroached upon by
> geniuses who creep
> 'out of every corner
> of the woodes and glennes'
> towards watercress and carrion.
>
> (WO 4–5)

Heaney offers us here a dense and complex vision. What the speaker sees is an image of the sixteenth-century English poet Edmund Spenser, who served as a minor colonial official in Ireland. Because of his service to the government, Spenser was able to acquire, cheaply, a large amount of property, including an estate at Kilcolman, in County Cork. While living at Kilcolman, Spenser wrote his famous poem *The Faerie Queene* and also composed a political treatise on Irish affairs, entitled *A View of the Present State of Ireland*, in which he advocated the deployment of extremely harsh measures against the native Irish. The Irish playwright Frank McGuinness has also been attracted to the figure of Spenser – in his play *Mutabilities* he imagines Shakespeare visiting Spenser at his Kilcolman estate.

As Michael Parker makes clear,[3] the connection back to Spenser is related to the central image of Heaney's poem. The colonizing schemes of the early modern era led to the extensive clearing of woodland areas, and we can presume that it is a piece of this cleared wood which emerges from the bog in the opening of the poem as 'A carter's trophy' to be 'Split for rafters'. 'Bog Oak', then, offers us a similar set of connections as 'At a Potato Digging'. Where the earlier poem suggests that, if we penetrate the surface of the contemporary rural landscape, we will find the unhealed wound of the Great Famine, 'Bog Oak' indicates that we can read the colonial history of the country within the grains of the retrieved timber. The sense of historical resonance is compounded by the quotation from Spenser's *View* which Heaney incorporates into his poem. In the treatise itself, the full passage appears as follows:

> Out of every corner of the woodes and glinnes they came creeping foorthe upon theyr handes, for theyr legges could not beare them; they looked like anatomyes of death, they spake like ghostes crying out of theyr graves; they did eate of the dead carrions, happy were they yf they could finde them, yea, and one another soone after, insoemuch as the very carcasses they spared not to scrape out of theyr graves; and yf they founde a plotte of water-cresses or shamrokes, there they flocked as to a feast . . .[4]

Spenser is writing of the famine in Munster which resulted from English campaigns against the Irish in the late sixteenth century, but we can hardly fail to hear an echo here, again, of the famine of the mid-nineteenth century, in which identical events played themselves out. Karl Marx has famously observed that 'all great world-historical facts and personages occur, as it were, twice. . . . the first time as tragedy, the second as farce',[5] but here we find history repeating itself not as tragedy and farce but as endlessly reiterated cycles of affliction and blight.

It is this sense of the repetition of cycles rooted deep in the past that attracted Heaney to Glob's book on *The Bog People*. What Glob offers is an image of a pre-Christian, northern European tribal society, in which ritual violence is a necessary part of the structure of life. Most of the Iron Age bodies recovered from the Jutland bogs and documented by Glob had been the victims of ritual killings, many of them having served as human sacrifices to the earth goddess Nerthus. Heaney detected a kinship between the pagan civilizations of Jutland and Ireland's own Celtic traditions and saw, as Michael Parker puts it, 'the fatal attraction of Nerthus liv[ing] on in such figures from the Nationalist pantheon as Kathleen ni Houlihan [Caitlín ní Houlihán], the Shan Van Vocht [Shean Bhean Bhocht], and Mother Ireland'.[6] Heaney himself affirms this view when, in conversation with John Haffenden, he observes that 'Irish catholicism is continuous with something older than christianity'.[7] In another interview, with Brian Donnelley, in 1977, Heaney articulated his sense of the force of the Iron Age narratives as a means of establishing a space in which it was possible for him to encounter contemporary atrocities which, otherwise, he did not feel he could adequately encompass within his poetry:

> My emotions, my feelings, whatever those instinctive energies are that have to be engaged for a poem, those energies quickened more when contemplating a victim, strangely, from 2000 years ago than they did from contemplating a man at the end of the road being swept into a plastic bag – I mean the barman at the end of our road tried to carry out a bomb and it blew up. Now there is of course something terrible about that, but somehow language, words didn't live in the way I think they have to live in a poem when they were hovering over that kind of horror and pity.[8]

Heaney makes his sense of the connections between Ireland and Jutland explicit in *Wintering Out* in a four-line poem entitled 'Nerthus'. The first brief stanza of the poem provides a symbolic image of the goddess – a rib of ash wood 'staked in peat' (*WO* 38). The rib is forked and is marked with an incision to represent the female genitalia: 'Its long grains gathering to the gouged split'. Neil Corcoran has observed of the second stanza of the poem – 'A seasoned, unsleeved taker of the weather, | Where kesh and loaning finger out to heather' – that it 'implicitly translates the goddess out of Iron Age Jutland into modern Northern Ireland [as] the landscape she stands in is defined in the terms of Northern dialect – "kesh", a causeway, and "loaning", an uncultivated space between fields'.[9] As Corcoran notes, the invocation of 'kesh' has a particular modern resonance, since it was at 'Long Kesh' (subseqently renamed the Maze Prison) that many of the North's political prisoners were held.

Heaney's first extended attempt at conflating his understanding of Glob's Jutland rituals with his own sense of mythic and modern Irish history comes in 'The Tollund Man' – the poem which precedes 'Nerthus' in *Wintering Out*. The 'Tollund Man' is one of the recovered bodies featured by Glob in his book. He was a victim sacrificed to Nerthus, in the hope of securing a good crop from the land, and it is in this sense that he is, as Heaney describes him, 'Bridegroom to the goddess' (*WO* 36). Heaney imagines the killing of the Tollund Man and his subsequent burial in the bog as a kind of violent love-making between victim and goddess, in which Nerthus, 'open[ing] her fen', preserves the victim's body by immersing it in her sexual 'dark juices'. When the Tollund Man is dug up, many centuries later, the turf-cutters discover 'His last gruel of winter seeds | Caked in his stomach'. As a sacrificial victim to the goddess of germination, then, he carries the potential of germination (his 'gruel of winter seeds') within himself, rather in the manner of the young fighters in 'Requiem for the Croppies' whose 'graves began to sprout with young barley, growing up from barley corn which [they] had carried in their pockets to eat while on the march' (*P*. 56).

In the second section of the poem, Heaney makes the connection between Jutland and Ireland explicit. If Jutland has had its victims, so too has Heaney's own native place. And in Ireland, too, the killings have a certain ritualistic dimension to them; Heaney recalls an incident in which the bodies of four young Catholics, murdered by Protestant militants, were dragged along a railway line in an act of mutilation:

> Tell-tale skin and teeth
> Flecking the sleepers

> Of four young brothers, trailed
> For miles along the lines.

> (*WO* 37)

Heaney imagines that, if he addresses a prayer to the Tollund Man ('risk[ing] blasphemy' as a Christian by aligning himself with the rituals of a pagan religion), then perhaps the potential for germination and regeneration inherent in the Tollund Man's sacrifice, and in his very body (buried with its freight of seed), might be released, not in the victim's native ancient Jutland, but in contemporary Ireland. It might 'make germinate | | The scattered, ambushed | Flesh' of the North's sacrificial victims.

In the final section of the poem, Heaney imagines paying a visit to the museum in Aarhus where the Tollund Man has been placed on display. Though the names of the region he passes through ('Tollund, Grabaulle, Nebelgard') will be alien to him, and the local language unintelligible, he fancies that, as an Irishman burdened with the weight of his country's history, he will feel a kinship with a landscape that has witnessed similar conflict and killings. As he writes in the precisely balanced closing stanza of the poem:

> Out there in Jutland
> In the old man-killing parishes
> I will feel lost,
> Unhappy and at home.

Heaney's most intense engagement with the Northern conflict occurs in his 1975 collection, *North*. Formally, much of *North* continues the trend towards shorter lines of verse, initiated in *Wintering Out*, as Heaney exploits further what Bernard O'Donoghue has referred to as 'the "artesian stanza", the short-lined poems that Heaney used to drill down metaphorically into his territory's and his consciousness's prehistory'.[10] Heaney observed at the time that he sought 'to take the English lyric and make it eat stuff that it has never eaten before ... like all the messy and, it would seem, incomprehensible obsessions in the North'.[11]

North is continuous with *Wintering Out* thematically as well as formally in that we are offered further bog poems in the collection, but Heaney also broadens the northern European connection as he recollects Ireland's Viking history and draws

40

upon the *Njal's Saga* as a source of mythological resonances. In 'Funeral Rites' Heaney begins with an autobiographical meditation on his experience of death as he grew up in the country. The funerals he remembers are not distinguished as being of particular people – the most specific detail he offers is that he lifted the coffins 'of dead relations' (*N*. 6). What dominates the opening section of the poem is a sense of the rituals and ceremonies which have been established in the family and the local community for encountering and assimilating the experience of death, for grieving and for resuming the flow of everyday life. Each funeral follows a routine pattern and the bodies of the dead take on a uniform appearance:

> their eyelids glistening,
> their dough-white hands
> shackled in rosary beads.
>
> Their puffed knuckles
> had unwrinkled, the nails
> were darkened, the wrists
> obediently sloped.

In this last image, we get a sense of death's having virtually been wrought into submission, as the disposition of the corpse conforms to the requirements of formal arrangement.

As the first section of the poem comes to an end, the sense of repetitive formality and religious ritual is reinforced: we are told that '*always*, in a corner, | the coffin lid, its nail-heads dressed | | with little gleaming crosses' (*N*. 7; emphasis added). The section concludes with a certain hint of regret, but with a definite sense of closure and completion:

> Dear soapstone masks,
> kissing their igloo brows
> had to suffice
>
> before the nails were sunk
> and the black glacier
> of each funeral
> pushed away.

There is a certain poignancy in the cold kiss delivered to the unyielding flesh before the coffin lid is hammered in place, but this is the way of '*each* funeral' and once the ritual is complete, death can be 'pushed away' and life resumed.

41

What the first section of the poem gives us, then, is a sense of death's having been encompassed by ritual in a way that makes the flow of life itself possible. The second section of the poem presents a stark contrast to this settled, cyclical world. In section II, we enter the contemporary realm of the Northern conflict, where the natural rhythms of the community are disrupted by the rise of sectarian violence, leading to what Heaney calls, in a disturbingly evocative phrase, 'neighbourly murder'. While the poet desires a reinstatement of old routines, observing

> we pine for ceremony,
> customary rhythms:
>
> the temperate footsteps
> of a cortège, winding past
> each blinded home

there is also a recognition here that the deep-running fissures of the conflict could never be healed by means of such easy, familiar pieties. Something more elemental, more deeply rooted in the historical fibres of the community, is required. It is for this reason that Heaney offers his vision of a single great funeral, arising out of the north and heading for 'the great chambers of Boyne' in the Irish midlands. Once again, what Heaney provides us with here is a densely interwoven set of compacted references. Just as the Nerthus cult of Glob's *Bog People* takes us back to pre-Christian Europe, so the burial chambers of the megalithic site of Newgrange, in the Boyne Valley, takes us back to pre-Christian Ireland. In the native Celtic religion, the Boyne was a sacred river, 'the fountain of all knowledge', and the Newgrange site itself was associated with Aengus, the Celtic god of love.[12] The Boyne has other associations too, however, since it was at the Battle of the Boyne in 1690 that the Catholic James II suffered a decisive defeat at the hands of the Protestant William of Orange, who would succeed him on the English throne. As the historian Roy Foster has observed: 'Ireland's peculiar conditions imposed an Irish configuration on the confrontation; in history and ballad ... the war ... was the last stand of Catholic Ireland against Protestant Ascendancy, imparting the epic aura still immortalized in the naïve art of Belfast gable-ends.'[13]

Heaney's restoration of the Boyne's Celtic associations thus takes us back past contemporary and historical conflict to a point in mythic history where reconciliation of enduring conflict might be effected. This point is made explicit in the closing section of the poem, where Heaney imagines the end of the funeral, with the mourners returning northwards. As they drive north, they pass by 'Strang and Carling fjords' (*N*. 8) – a reference to Ireland's Viking history, detected in the Irish place-names of 'Strangford' and 'Carlingford'. This memory of Ireland's Norse connections summons up in turn, in the closing stanzas of the poem, an uncharacteristic moment of quiescence and harmony from the epic Icelandic *Njal's Saga*. Heaney imagines the Irish victims his poem has carried to rest in Newgrange as being 'disposed like Gunnar' (*N*. 9) – himself a victim of the *Saga*'s remorseless cycles of revenge. The aftermath of Gunnar's death is untypical in the story and has a particular resonance for the situation in Ireland. He lay, we are told, 'beautiful | inside his burial mound, | though dead by violence | | and unavenged'. Gunnar thus lies at rest, even though his allies have effected no vengeance killing against his enemies in reprisal for his death. His story thus provides an instance of the cycle of revenge killings being broken and offers hope for Ireland at a time when the cycle of sectarian murders appears interminable. The poem ends with an image of peaceful resolution, as Gunnar rises within his tomb, serene and untroubled:

> Men said that he was chanting
> verses about honour
> and that four lights burned
>
> in corners of the chamber:
> which opened then, as he turned
> with joyful face
> to look at the moon.

The vision which Heaney offers here of easy reconciliation and sublime peacefulness is, however, not sustained throughout the volume as a whole. Much more characteristic of *North*'s troubled register and remit is a piece such as the much discussed bog poem 'Punishment', where Heaney engages with the contemporary conflict through the lens of his trope of bog retrieval. As in the case of 'The Tollund Man', Heaney's point of departure here is again a photograph from Glob's *The Bog People*. In this case, it is a picture of a young woman who had likely been

43

shorn, stripped, killed, and thrown into the bog as a punishment for adultery. 'Punishment' is, throughout, an uneasy poem, which seems deeply uncertain both of its own motives and of its ability to achieve any point of equilibrium or certainty. This uneasiness is registered in the opening stanzas of the work, when the poet begins by expressing a sense of identification and empathy with the victim, but very quickly becomes a voyeur (as he explicitly admits in a later stanza of the poem), exercising his male power to take pleasure in the woman's exposed and subjected body:

> I can feel the tug
> of the halter at the nape
> of her neck, the wind
> on her naked front.
>
> It blows her nipples
> to amber beads,
> it shakes the frail rigging
> of her ribs.

(N. 30)

The conflict indicated here is both given further expression and compounded later in the piece, in the poet's direct address to the dead woman. 'My poor scapegoat', he writes, 'I almost love you | but would have cast, I know, | the stones of silence' (N. 31). Heaney conflates pagan and Christian mythologies here, as the story of the Jutland victim is combined with the story of the woman caught in adultery included in the Christian Gospel According to St John. The poet indicates that, his attraction to the woman notwithstanding, he would have been complicit in her death, if not directly, then certainly by failing to raise his voice in support of her or in protest at her punishment. In the closing stanzas of the poem, this sense of troubled complicity in an act of violence is extended from its immediate focus in the poet's contemplation of this Iron Age victim to the circumstances of the contemporary conflict in Northern Ireland, as the poet characterizes himself as one who has

> stood dumb
> when your betraying sisters,
> cauled in tar,
> wept by the railings,

who would connive
in civilized outrage
yet understand the exact,
and tribal, intimate revenge.

Like 'Funeral Rites', this poem too takes up the question of revenge. But the revenge in question is effected within the community itself, rather than between two opposing communities. The woman victim retrieved from the bog provides an image for those young Catholic women in Heaney's own Northern Ireland subjected to 'tarring and feathering' by members of their own community. The punishment was most often inflicted on those who became involved with members of the British Army. Like Glob's female victim, the women typically had their heads shaved, before having hot tar and feathers poured over them and being left tied up in a public place, as an act of ritual humiliation.

The poet's response to the contemporary punishment, like his response to its Iron Age analogue, is conflicted and ambiguous. On the one hand, he 'connive[s] | in civilized outrage', deploying the kind of non-commital liberal attitude that he anatomizes later in *North*, in 'Whatever You Say Say Nothing': ' "Oh, it's disgraceful, surely, I agree," | "Where's it going to end?" "It's getting worse" ' (*N*. 52). On the other hand, he again finds himself complicit in the act of retribution, as he admits that he is able to understand (and, by extension, in some measure to sympathize with) the rationale for the punitive act. The punishment is characterized as 'exact | and tribal' – it is presented as being precisely calibrated – 'justified' in a literal sense – and as having its roots deep in the ancestral mindset of the community, being therefore in some sense inevitable and unavoidable. Conor Cruise O'Brien, the Irish scholar, politician, and controversialist, regarded the poem as offering a profoundly depressing analysis of the Irish situation when he reviewed *North* in the *Listener*:

> It is the word 'exact' that hurts most: Seamus Heaney has so greatly earned the right to use this word that to see him use it as he does here opens up a sort of chasm. But then, of course, that is what he is about. The word 'exact' fits the situation as it is felt to be: and it is because it fits and because other situations, among the rival population, turn on similarly oiled pivots, that hope succumbs. I have read many pessimistic analyses of 'Northern Ireland', but none that has the bleak conclusiveness of these poems.[14]

45

The ambivalence which Heaney displays here about the exactness of tribal violence is registered elsewhere in the first part of *North* also. In the closing section of 'Kinship', for example, Heaney calls upon the Roman historian, Tacitus, to be a witness to the situation in Ireland. Tacitus mentions Ireland in his *Agricola* and he devotes a chapter to the cult of Nerthus in his *Germania*. Once again blending the contemporary with the mythical, Heaney, addressing Tacitus, offers him material for another study of the Nerthus cult. 'Our mother ground' he writes 'is sour with the blood | of her faithful, | they lie gargling | in her sacred heart'. Where the original devotees of Nerthus offered sacrificial victims to her in the hope of increasing the fertility of the land, here the glut of corpses serves merely to sour the soil. In closing the poem, Heaney exhorts Tacitus to 'Read the inhumed faces'

> of casualty and victim;
> report us fairly,
> how we slaughter
> for the common good
>
> and shave the heads
> of the notorious,
> how the goddess swallows
> our love and terror.

(N. 38–9)

Blake Morrison has observed of these lines that they are one of the moments in *North* where, 'like it or not', Heaney's 'poetry grants sectarian killing in Northern Ireland a historical respectability which it is not usually granted in day-to-day journalism: precedent becomes, if not a justification, then at least an "explanation" '.[15] While one might quibble with the details of Morrison's judgement here (not least with the faith he seems to place in 'day-to-day journalism'), nevertheless, his broader point is well taken: as in the case of 'Punishment', the violence here appears to have a certain air of inevitability about it. The source of the current troubles, Heaney seems to be suggesting, lies deep in mythic history, where ineluctable cycles have been set in motion. In a dangerous elision, 'love' and 'terror' seem also to become inextricably entwined, as the goddess of the earth 'swallows' both without distinction.

'Punishment' and 'Kinship' both offer gendered images of the Irish conflict. Female figures are presented in the poems as

46

analogues for the victims of the conflict and the conflict's source respectively. As the first section of *North* draws to a close, Heaney offers a further gendered image of the situation in the poems 'Ocean's Love to Ireland' and 'Act of Union'. The first of these poems returns us to the early colonial era which we saw Heaney explore in 'Bog Oak', when he presented us with an image of Edmund Spenser 'dreaming sunlight' as the starving Irish crept out of the woods. In 'Ocean's Love to Ireland' Heaney turns to a contemporary and friend of Spenser's, Walter Ralegh, who, like Spenser, had extensive colonial interests in Ireland. Heaney's poem takes as its point of departure both Ralegh's own poetic fragment 'The Ocean's Love to Cynthia' and an anecdote from Ralegh's biography concerning his raping of a young woman. This story is related in the first section of the poem and then, in the second section, Heaney goes on to make reference to Ralegh's presence (together with Spenser) at the mass execution of a small Spanish force which had landed in the south-west of Ireland. The soldiers were put to death, despite having sur- rendered to the English (Spenser offers a justification for the killings in his *View of the Present State of Ireland*). In the third and final section of the poem, Heaney conflates these sexual and colonial anecdotes to suggest that Ireland, in its colonial predica- ment, is in a similar position to the victim of Ralegh's act of rape. A personified Ireland merges with the figure of the assaulted woman in the final stanza:

> She fades from their somnolent clasp
> Into ringlet-breath and dew,
> The ground possessed and repossessed.

> (*N.* 41)

In 'Act of Union' this metaphorical imagining of Ireland as the victim of English sexual assault is made even more explicit. Where in 'Ocean's Love to Ireland', Heaney describes Ralegh as 'back[ing] the maid to a tree | as Ireland is backed to England' (*N.* 40), in the second poem of the pair, England is presented as 'the tall kingdom over [Ireland's] shoulder' (*N.* 43), who pene- trates the quiescent, female Ireland, engendering, in the process, the colony of the North. As the metaphorized England tells Ireland: 'His parasitical | And ignorant little fists already | Beat at your borders and I know they're cocked | At me across the water.' The poem gloomily can envision no resolution to the conflict, as England comments in its closing lines:

> No treaty
> I foresee will salve completely your tracked
> And stretchmarked body, the big pain
> That leaves you raw, like opened ground, again.

(*N.* 43–4)

Despite the delicate aspirations and hopefulness of 'Funeral Rites', then, it is, as we have seen Conor Cruise O'Brien indicate, this tone of despair that predominates in *North*, both throughout the mythologizing, historicizing poems of the first section and the more contemporary pieces of the short second section, where *Wintering Out*'s poem of dedication is repeated as the closing section of 'Whatever You Say Say Nothing' and, in 'Orange Drums, Tyrone, 1966', the Protestant drummer beats out an anti-Catholic rhythm that sets the air vibrating:

> To every cocked ear, expert in its greed,
> His battered signature subscribes 'No Pope'.
> The goatskin's sometimes plastered with his blood.
> The air is pounding like a stethoscope.

(*N.* 62)

This trajectory of despair is registered in the poems placed at the opening and the conclusion of part one of the book. Both poems centre on the mythical conflict between Hercules and Antaeus. Antaeus draws his strength from the land and is renewed by the land every time he touches it. In the first of the two poems he is triumphant and unassailable, never having been defeated. In the second poem, however, he faces a Hercules who 'has the measure | of resistance and black powers | feeding off the territory' (*N.* 46) and who, therefore, raises him off the land and holds him tightly as his strength drains away, finally crushing him to death. In both poems, Antaeus serves as a figure for the native communities who opposed the advance of colonialism throughout the world. The struggle of these traditional, pastoral, earthbound societies was, Heaney suggests, always doomed to failure, as they faced an adversary whose technological advantage and whose world-view always outstripped and exceeded that of the communities who resisted them.[16]

48

Both these poems register a note of pessimism and exhaustion which resonates with the dominant register of *North*. Its occasional moments of mythically imagined optimism notwithstanding, the volume, taken as a whole, is brooding, distraught, and deeply conflicted. It indicates anxieties and uncertainties which would play themselves out more explicitly in the volumes that succeeded it.

3

'I hear again the sure confusing drum': Reversions and Revisions

Neil Rhodes provides an astute reading of 'Act of Union' in 'Bridegrooms to the Goddess', where he notes that a longer version of the poem was published under the title 'A New Life' in the *Listener* in 1973. In this version, the occasion of the poem is Marie Heaney's third pregnancy and the poem 'ends in family peace, the crying baby calmed by mother and father, "[t]he triangle of forces solved in love"'. Rhodes registers both the motivation for the changed ending as it appeared in *North* and the effect which the change has on the poem:

> The fading out of the original occasion for the poem and the substitution of the copulation metaphor for the 'new life' of the first title, is an attempt to wrench it back into allegory, but the poem remains a mess. To call it a mess, though, is less to criticize Heaney than to regret the degree of public expectation and pressure responsible for it . . . Behind the two versions of 'Act of Union' you can almost hear the admonitory whispers, 'the personal is political.'[1]

In the wake of Heaney's engagement with the political in *North* and elsewhere, the 'admonitory whispers' – and more directly spoken admonishing rebukes – came thick and fast.

Thus, in an article on Heaney entitled 'The Trouble with Seamus', James Simmons castigates the poet for offering the reader, in *North*, a 'barren nationalism [that] descends into vanity and

50

self-pity'.[2] Edna Longley, in a more substantial consideration of Heaney's work in *Poetry in the Wars*, provides much the same assessment, and in a chapter of the book entitled 'Poetry and Politics in Northern Ireland' she suggests that 'poetry and politics, like church and state, should be separated. And for the same reasons: mysteries distort the rational processes which ideally prevail in social relations; while ideologies confiscate the poet's special passport to *terra incognita*.'[3]

For Simmons and Longley, Heaney indulges too much in politics, or rather, perhaps, indulges in politics of the wrong kind. Other commentators on Heaney's poems on the Irish conflict – especially those included in *North* – have, however, taken a rather different line. Desmond Fennell, for example, in a belligerent but sometimes insightful pamphlet entitled *Whatever You Say, Say Nothing*, observes of Heaney's poems about the North that they say 'nothing, plainly or figuratively'

> about the war, about any of the three main parties to it, or about the issues at stake. Nor, indeed – quite apart from 'saying' – is anything *suggested* about the war except that it is sad, rooted in history, often ruthless, and connected with the oppression of the poet's people and sacrifice to the goddess. Of course, in the minds of readers, especially if they are at a distance from the scene, the poems about prehistoric bodies in a Jutland bog, and about particulars of the Northern Ireland war, may fuse together as 'poems about irrational violence'; and that is certainly their collective suggestion. But Heaney says nothing about irrational violence, and all he *suggests* about it, generically, is that it is evil and sad: an insight which we hardly need to read poetry for.[4]

What Fennell is objecting to here is what he perceives as a lack of true political engagement in Heaney's poems. Heaney, he proposes, does not address the particularities of the current political situation, but rather offers us, instead, anodyne observations cloaked in the mythic trappings of pagan ritual. Fennell points here to a critique of Heaney's 'political' poems which is most cogently expressed in the analyses of Ciarán Carson and David Lloyd. Though they come to the poetry from quite different perspectives, what both Carson and Lloyd object to in Heaney's work is what they regard as its dangerous conflation of myth and history, such that, again, the political particularities of the situations Heaney writes about become obscured. Reviewing

North in the *Honest Ulsterman*, Carson observes (with particular reference to 'Punishment'):

> It is as if he is saying, suffering like this is natural; these things have always happened; they happened then, they happen now, and that is sufficient ground for understanding and absolution. It is as if there never were and never will be any political consequences of such acts; they have been removed to the realm of sex, death and inevitability.[5]

Carson's point here is that in assimilating contemporary political actions – killings, punishments, mutilations – to a mythic past, Heaney in some sense 'naturalizes' these actions, makes them seem somehow inevitable, part of an immemorial, tribal cycle that cannot be broken, or even challenged, and, in the process, Heaney lifts these actions and events out of their actual historical and political context, leaving us no sense of *how* or *why* they have happened. Lacking such an understanding, we cannot see our way to envisioning a solution to the crisis in political or truly social terms. The only kind of solution that is possible within this paradigm is something like that offered in poems such as 'Funeral Rites' or 'Broagh', where communities are brought together in highly aestheticized ideal gestures of reconciliation – united by a trope out of the *Njal's Saga*, or by the ability to pronounce the final phoneme of a local place-name. As David Lloyd observes in ' "Pap for the Dispossessed": Seamus Heaney and the Poetics of Identity' – one of the most penetrating and compelling critiques of Heaney's work – Heaney's typical poetic paradigm serves 'to reduce history to myth, furnishing an aesthetic resolution to conflicts constituted in quite specific historical junctures by rendering disparate events as symbolic moments expressive of an underlying continuity of identity'.[6]

While Carson's and Lloyd's criticisms are perceptive and valid, it should also be noted that Heaney is himself anxiously alert to the problematics of writing poems about the Irish political situation.[7] Much of his poetry is scored with the apprehension that his sense of responsibility as a Northern Irish poet brings to him – a responsibility felt all the more keenly because of Heaney's profound attraction to the work of the Russian poet Osip Mandelstam, who suffered greatly at the hands of the Soviet authorities because of his fidelity to his poetic vision. In the sequence 'A Northern Hoard' in *Wintering Out*, Heaney worries again and again about the issue of whether the poet can ever have any kind of effective role in the face of intense suffering, as he asks himself such questions as 'Why do I unceasingly I arrive late to condone I infected sutures I and ill-knit bone?' (*WO* 30) and 'What do I say if they wheel out their dead?' (*WO* 31). Repeatedly he wonders just what the poet has to offer in circumstances of overwhelming grief and loss.

Heaney's sense of conflict over his own position is clearly focused in 'Exposure', the poem which brings *North* to a close. The title is ironically ambiguous, referring at one and the same time to his celebrity status as a public poet who has received much media exposure and also to his sense of vulnerability (of being 'exposed') as someone who has attempted to engage with the political conflict and who, as a result, bears the weight of his own community's expectations as well as the resentments of some of those in the North who are faithful to an opposing tradition. There may also be a hint in the title of a certain degree of anxiety on Heaney's part that his poems and public life may lead to exposure of another kind – that he may be revealed as being not truly faithful to what he purports to represent or support, or that he may not live up to the expectations of his own community, who would fashion him as a public spokesman of a particular kind – in short, that he may be exposed as a 'fraud'.

The poem begins by locating the poet geographically, as he opens with the line 'It is December in Wicklow' (*N*. 66). County Wicklow is south of Dublin, in the Republic of Ireland. Heaney and his family had moved to a cottage in Glanmore, in Wicklow, in August 1972. Because he was so prominent a public figure, the move was much commented upon, with the Unionist *Protestant Telegraph* rejoicing in the fact that 'the well-known papist propagandist' was on his way to 'his spiritual home in the popish republic'. In an interview with Seamus Deane in the *New York Times Review* some years later, Heaney recalled his own sense of ambivalence about the move: 'Going to the South was perhaps emblematic for me and was certainly so for some of the people I knew. To the Unionists it looked like a betrayal of the Northern thing. Living in the South, I found myself lonelier, imaginatively.'[8]

In the poem itself, Heaney again troubles over the role of the poet and his political responsibilities. Rooted in his mundane rural home he imagines a hero of mythical proportions who might make a stand for his oppressed people, like David challenging Goliath (the sort of gesture that we imagine might be approved of by Desmond Fennell):

> I walk through damp leaves,
> Husks, the spent flukes of autumn,
>
> Imagining a hero
> On some muddy compound,
> His gift like a slingstone
> Whirled for the desperate.

But it is clear to Heaney in the poem that he himself is not the kind of poet who can play the part of such a David and, in any case, in an earlier poem in the collection – 'The Unacknowledged Legislator's Dream' (the title is derived from Shelley's observation that poets are the unacknowledged legislators of the world) – he had interrogated the notion that a poet in the mould of the heroic David could ever offer anything more than a kind of brief and ineffectual display of political bravado. In the poem, the figure of the poet sinks his 'crowbar in a chink . . . under the masonry of state and statute' (N. 50), but, while his showy gestures of rebellion elicit a cheer from his 'wronged people [in] their cages', he finds himself quickly captured and, imprisoned by the authorities, discovers that he is regarded with a certain indulgent good humour by the agents of the system he has sought to overthrow:

> The commandant motions me to be seated. 'I am
> honoured to add a poet to our list.' He is amused
> and genuine. 'You'll be safer here, anyhow.'

The machinery of state is, finally, untroubled by the poet's grand gesture of insurrection.

Unable or unwilling to fulfil the role of an insurgent David, Heaney in 'Exposure' puzzles over his position as someone who lies outside the easy categorizations of the political realm, as he writes: 'I am neither internee nor informer; | An inner émigré, grown long-haired | And thoughtful' (N. 67). He is, in other words, neither a victim of the political situation, an emblematic member of his people ('internees' were suspected militant activists who were imprisoned by the authorities without trial), nor is he a traitor to his people (an 'informer', who betrays members of his own community to the authorities). In a phrase derived from the old Soviet regime (specifically, from the official designation of the imprisoned Mandelstam), he presents himself instead as 'an inner émigré' – someone finally disjoined from the political situation while still being subject to it.

As the poem draws to a conclusion, Heaney offers a further set of images intended to indicate his sense of his own situation, describing himself as 'a wood-kerne'

> Escaped from the massacre,
> Taking protective colouring
> From bole and bark, feeling
> Every wind that blows;
>
> Who, blowing up these sparks
> For their meagre heat, have missed
> The once-in-a-lifetime portent,
> The comet's pulsing rose.

In one sense, these stanzas seem like an appropriate conclusion to *North*, in that they appear to indicate a certain exhaustion with *North*'s greater project of attempting to come to terms with the troubled political situation in Ireland. Having ventured into the conflict, Heaney at the last imagines himself as a native soldier (a 'wood-kerne') who has managed to escape from the scene of hostilities, receding into a natural, rural world. To this extent, the poem seems to signal a kind of 'retreat'.

The closing lines of the poem pick up on an image that Heaney evokes earlier in the piece, when he writes that

> A comet that was lost
> Should be visible at sunset,
> Those million tons of light
> Like a glimmer of haws and rose-hips,
>
> And I sometimes see a falling star.
> If I could come on meteorite!
>
> (*N*. 66)

In asserting, at the close of the poem, that he has missed the 'comet's pulsing rose', Heaney may well be ruefully acknowledging a certain sense of having failed, in *North*, adequately to trace the large-scale outlines of his country's and his community's predicament. But there is also, we may feel, a sense in the poem as a whole that a certain fidelity to the 'meagre heat' of small-scale particularities is, in itself, both more necessary and more valid than the kind of large-scale mythic exegesis that he elsewhere attempts. In this sense, we might say that Heaney himself discovers within his work the very critique of his poetry which commentators such as Lloyd and Carson have offered. As in the case of 'The Unacknowledged Legislator's Dream', where Heaney queries the effectiveness of ostentatious political/ poetic gestures, here too he seems to question the efficacy of attempting (as he does in so many of the poems of *North*) to construct grand political and mythic narratives, whose overarching trajectory fully accounts for the contemporary conflict.

Such a view of Heaney's position in 'Exposure' suggests that what he seeks, in Glanmore, is less a retreat from the political situation as such than one from what he calls in the poem 'The diamond absolutes' of easy political certainties and all-encompassing historical and mythical narratives. Echoing somewhat the sentiments of Simmons, Carson, and Lloyd, Maurice Harmon has observed that

> The metaphor of ceremony permeates *North*, a collection deeply concerned with the violence of Northern Ireland. The poems do not confront that violence. They do not speak of individual pain or individual outrage. Instead Heaney adopts a communal response. Whatever personal feelings he has about death and suffering are deflected into large, ceremonial gestures.[9]

If 'Exposure' signals a potential turning-away from such an expansive ceremonial mode, that reorientation is confirmed in the immediate successors to *North* – *Field Work* (1979) and, especially, *Station Island* (1984). In many of the poems in these two volumes Heaney turns precisely to the issue of 'individual pain [and] individual outrage'. Across these volumes he increasingly places under scrutiny the inherited political, cultural, and religious truisms of his community and the dominant register of many of the poems in the two volumes is interrogative. The shift in perception and approach is mirrored in an accompanying shift in poetic form. Where, in *Wintering Out* and *North*, Heaney had adopted the narrow 'artesian stanza' – a form with which he sought, metaphorically, to drill down into the prehistoric sources of conflict – from *Field Work* onwards the poetic line fills out again, expanding to carry the weight of interrogation.

We should note that Heaney does continue to feel a responsibility to speak for his community in these volumes. In *Field Work*'s 'The Toome Road', in particular, he registers a sense of bitterness at the continuing presence of British troops in Northern Ireland. In the poem, he imagines an encounter between a Northern Irish farmer and a British Army convoy, on patrol along a stretch of country road. The farmer asserts his sense of indignation at what he perceives as this foreign intrusion into a landscape in which he is deeply rooted as a native. 'How long were they approaching down my roads | As if they owned them?' he asks, and he goes on to assert his own sense of connection with the land:

> I had rights-of-way, fields, cattle in my keeping,
> Tractors hitched to buckrakes in open sheds,
> Silos, chill gates, wet slates, the greens and reds
> Of outhouse roofs.

> (*FW* 15)

By the end of the poem, the British soldiers are addressed as 'charioteers', thus becoming conflated with their imperial precursors from the Roman Empire. The speaker in the poem offers them a defiant declaration:

> O charioteers, above your dormant guns,
> It stands here still, stands vibrant as you pass,
> The invisible, untoppled omphalos.

The implication is that, just as the Roman Empire has declined and fallen, so too the resources of the local community – the 'omphalos' (a word which Heaney associates with the pumping of water from a communal well – see *Preoccupations*, 17) – will ultimately outlast the colonial regime.

'The Toome Road' seems to suggest that the defeat of colonialism will be effected through the feat of simple endurance. Elsewhere in *Field Work* Heaney engages with the consequences of a more militant form of nationalism and of political violence generally. 'After a Killing', the first section of 'Triptych', was written in the wake of the assassination of Christopher Ewart-Biggs, the British ambassador to Ireland, whose car was blown up by the IRA in 1976. The poem is haunted by the presence, in the first stanza, of two shadowy gunmen:

There they were, as if our memory hatched them,
As if the unquiet founders walked again:
Two young men with rifles on the hill,
Profane and bracing as their instruments.

(FW 12)

The stanza is curiously ambiguous. Twice in the first two lines
we are offered the uncertainty of statements introduced with
the words 'as if'. The young men appear 'as if' they have been
summoned out of memory (presumably a kind of 'communal memory', since the poem invokes 'we' rather than 'I'); they
appear 'as if' they might be the returned spirits of those whose
struggle led to the founding of the nation state. It is not clear,
then, whether Heaney feels that the community is in sympathy
with these militants, nor is it clear whether he feels that there
is a clear line of continuity between earlier armed struggles and
the violent campaign being pursued in contemporary Ireland
(the question of whether the contemporary IRA is continuous
with the IRA whose 1916 uprising served partly to break the
link with Britain has always been a contentious issue in Ireland).
The sense of ambiguity is sustained in the closing line of the
stanza, where the gunmen are seen as 'profane' and 'bracing'.
'Profane' suggests that they are unholy, polluted, that they
engage in acts of defilement and violation. But 'bracing' conjures
up images of strength, vigour, and defiance. Similarly, in the
concluding line of the stanza, the rifles which the gunmen carry
are described as 'instruments' (rather than, for instance,
weapons), suggesting precision, craft, and skill rather than
violence and murder.

Heaney seems unwilling to surrender his ambivalence over
the course of 'Triptych'. In the second section of the poem, 'Sibyl',
we are offered powerful images of desecration and its consequences and enjoined to a discipline of pardon and mercy, as
when the section's *aisling*-like (dreamlike) figure foresees ineluctable decline for her people unless

forgiveness finds its nerve and voice,
Unless the helmeted and bleeding tree
Can green and open buds like infants' fists
And the fouled magma incubate

Bright nymphs.

(FW 13)

At the same time, however, there seems to be an unwillingness on the part of the poet fully to adopt this position in the face of provocation and oppression. The third section of the poem, 'At the Water's Edge', struggles to establish itself in the idyllic natural world of the sacred islands of Northern Ireland's Lough Erne, but the insular tranquillity is troubled by 'the thick rotations | Of an army helicopter patrolling' (*FW* 14). As in the case of 'The Toome Road', an alien element intrudes itself into the natural landscape. In the final stanza of the poem, the sound of the rotor blades summons up memories of another helicopter, this time hovering over a political protest – a march to mark public outrage at the killing of thirteen unarmed Civil Rights demonstrators by the British Army on 'Bloody Sunday' in January 1972:

> How we crept before we walked! I remembered
> The helicopter shadowing our march at Newry,
> The scared, irrevocable steps.

The march is a sign of defiance in the face of the shadowing helicopter, but we might wonder exactly what it is that Heaney is signalling when he writes 'How we crept before we walked!' What is 'creeping' and what is 'walking'?[10] The tentative steps of the protest march are 'irrevocable': in the wake of the protest there is no going back to an attitude of submissiveness in the face of oppression. But we might ask ourselves, again, whether the defiance of the protest march is continuous with the 'bracing' defiance of the gunmen with whom Heaney opens the poem. Indeed, we might ask whether, ironically, resistance to oppression is to be seen as running legitimately to the politically motivated killing that provides the occasion for the poem. Later in his career, in his Nobel lecture, 'Crediting Poetry', Heaney engages with this very kind of ambivalence:

> I remember . . . shocking myself with a thought I had about [a] friend who was imprisoned in the seventies upon suspicion of having been involved with a political murder: I shocked myself by thinking that even if he were guilty, he might still perhaps be helping the future to be born, breaking the repressive forms and liberating new potential in the only way that worked, that is to say the violent way – which therefore became, by extension, the right way. (*OG* 456–7)

This thought, Heaney insists, however, is merely a fleeting one – 'a moment of exposure to interstellar cold, a reminder of the scary element, both inner and outer, in which human beings must envisage and conduct their lives' (*OG* 457).

To return to the poetry itself, we can see Heaney beginning to address these issues in 'Casualty', another of *Field Work*'s poems to take up the question of the aftermath of the Bloody Sunday killings. Neil Corcoran has observed that to 'the republican or nationalist mind' 'Casualty' is

> a scandalous poem, one that proposes an image of divorce even in the act of memorializing the worst of the atrocities perpetrated by the British Army in Ulster: the one poem of Heaney's which explicitly includes Bloody Sunday is an elegy not for its thirteen dead, but for the one 'Casualty' – that neutrally exculpating, statistical term of the military strategist – killed in reprisal.[11]

The central figure presented in this poem is Louis O'Neill, a Catholic fisherman who was a neighbour and acquaintance of Heaney's in the North. O'Neill was, as the poem puts it, 'blown to bits' in an IRA pub bombing, carried out in reprisal for Bloody Sunday. The IRA had imposed a curfew on the Catholic community, but O'Neill had defied it, searching out an open pub in which to enjoy his usual evening's drinking. Heaney imagines O'Neill at the moment of the explosion

> as he turned
> In that bombed offending place,
> Remorse fused with terror
> In his still knowable face,
> His cornered outfaced stare
> Blinding in the flash.
>
> (*FW* 22–3)

In contrast with 'Triptych', where the victim whose death prompts the poem never appears and is never even evoked, in 'Casualty' we are presented with a vivid image of the victim, both in the course of his life and in the last moment before that life is destroyed. More than this, he is allowed a voice in the poem, as Heaney imagines himself being gently interrogated by the murdered O'Neill:

> How culpable was he
> That night when he broke

Our tribe's complicity?
'Now you're supposed to be
An educated man,'
I hear him say. 'Puzzle me
The right answer to that one.'

(*FW* 23)

O'Neill's death forces Heaney to confront the deep moral conflicts to which the campaign of violence gives rise. He has no
answer to offer O'Neill, but he welcomes the process of interrogation the fisherman provokes, as he addresses O'Neill directly
in the closing lines of the poem: 'Dawn-sniffing revenant, |
Plodder through midnight rain, | Question me again' (*FW* 24).

Elsewhere in *Field Work*, and subsequently in *Station Island*,
Heaney memorializes other victims of the Northern Irish conflict. Unlike the highly mythologized victims of *North*, many
of these figures are presented, like Louis O'Neill, in the full
flow of a life interrupted by an unexpected and brutal death.
'A Postcard from North Antrim' provides a vivid sketch of Sean
Armstrong, a friend of Heaney's from Queen's University, who
had spent some time in a Sausalito commune, but who returned
to Belfast to become involved in social work. In the first three
stanzas Heaney offers Armstrong a selection of good-humoured
postcard images of his own life. When Armstrong's death comes,
in the concluding lines of the fourth stanza, it is unexpected and
shocking:

You were the clown
Social worker of the town
Until your candid forehead stopped
A pointblank teatime bullet.

(*FW* 19)

The insertion of the homely 'teatime' between 'pointblank' and
'bullet' serves to render the killing all the more disturbing and
affecting, and, though the second half of the poem returns to
images of social occasions shared with Armstrong, the whole
atmosphere of the poem, as Michael Parker ably indicates,
has been tainted by the brutal murder. Even the wine which
Armstrong freely distributes at the end is reminiscent of his
own spilt blood.[12]

Another victim to be memorialized in *Field Work* is Heaney's own second cousin Colum McCartney, whose murder by loyalist gunmen is recalled in 'The Strand at Lough Beg'. Like much of *Field Work*, this poem is greatly indebted to the work of Dante, especially his *Divine Comedy*. The poem opens with an epigraph from the *Purgatorio* and ends with an image which is also borrowed from the same source. In Dante's poem, Virgil, the poet's guide, washes the grime of Hell from off the poet's face before he moves on to the next stage of his journey and enters Purgatory: 'When we were at a part where the dew resists the sun and, being in the shade, is little dispersed, my Master gently laid both hands outspread on the grass. I, therefore, aware of his purpose, reached toward him my tear-stained cheeks and on them he wholly restored that colour which Hell had hidden in me.'[13] Heaney conceives of performing the same ritual of purification on the body of his murdered cousin, as he pictures himself finding McCartney 'With blood and roadside muck in [his] hair and eyes' (*FW* 18). Heaney imagines himself

> kneel . . . in brimming grass
> And gather up cold handfuls of the dew
> To wash you, cousin. I dab you clean with moss
> Fine as the drizzle out of a low cloud.

At the end of the purification ritual in the *Purgatorio*, Virgil girds the poet with rushes which 'spring up again immediately in the place where he had plucked' them. Likewise, Heaney plaits 'green scapulars' for his cousin from 'rushes that shoot green again'. The poem ends, then, with images of purification and renewal.

In some respects we might feel that 'The Strand at Lough Beg' has more in common with the mythologizing poems of *North* than it has with its companion pieces on political violence in *Field Work*. We might recall, for instance, the image of the murdered woman in 'Punishment', her body metaphorized into an aesthetic object, as the wind 'blows her nipples | to amber beads' (*N*. 30). Similarly the consolation offered here – like the consolations and reconciliations offered in *North* – is metaphorical and highly mythologized. Heaney himself picks up on this very issue when he returns to consider McCartney's death once more in *Station Island*, a volume more searching and more sceptical than its immediate predecessor. In section VIII of the collection's title poem, McCartney, like Louis O'Neill in 'Casualty', is granted a voice to question the poet. As he first encounters the 'bleeding, pale-faced boy, plastered in mud' (*SI* 82), the poet is unable immediately to recognize him, and McCartney sharply prompts his memory by reminding him of where he was – at Jerpoint Abbey, Kilkenny, in the south of Ireland – on the day when his cousin was murdered:

> You were there with poets when you got the word
> and stayed there with them, while your own flesh and blood
> was carted to Bellaghy from the Fews.
> They showed more agitation at the news
> than you did.

The poet attempts to defend himself for pledging a greater fidelity to the world of poetry than to the actuality of his cousin's death. As part of his defence, he offers McCartney an aesthetic image and a metaphor for his own reaction: 'I kept seeing a grey stretch of Lough Beg | and the strand empty at daybreak. | I felt like the bottom of a dried-up lake' (*SI* 83). On hearing this, McCartney presses home his attack – it is precisely this metaphorizing tendency, which leads away from the particular to the aesthetic, that he objects to in Heaney's handling of his death in 'The Strand at Lough Beg':

> 'You saw that, and you wrote that – not the fact,
> You confused evasion and artistic tact.
> The Protestant who shot me through the head
> I accuse directly, but indirectly, you
>
> . . . .
>
> ... you whitewashed ugliness and drew
> the lovely blinds of the *Purgatorio*
> and saccharined my death with morning dew.'

Again like Louis O'Neill, the figure of McCartney here forces Heaney to reconsider his allegiances and responsibilities as a poet. The section of 'Station Island' dedicated to McCartney is typical of the sequence as a whole, which is very much concerned with issues of reappraisal and reassessment and with the interrogation of old beliefs and fidelities.

'Station Island' takes its basic conceit from the tradition of pilgrimage literature associated with an island in Lough Derg

63

in County Donegal. The island itself has strong associations with Saint Patrick, and the pilgrimage involves a three-day stay, during which time the pilgrim fasts and prays, in addition to completing, barefoot, nine circuits of the island. A number of Irish authors have written about the pilgrimage experience and Heaney fits his own narrative within that literary tradition.

In 'Station Island' Heaney comes face to face with the ideologies of his community and reassesses his own position in relation to them. As in the case of *Field Work*, Heaney is greatly indebted to Dante and, like the *Divine Comedy*, 'Station Island' is structured as a series of encounters with the ghosts of dead figures who are either known to Heaney personally or have been important to him as a writer. The first two encounters take place before the poet arrives on the island itself and the final encounter also occurs on the mainland, as he steps off the boat returning him from the island.

In the first of the encounters, the poet comes upon an old County Derry neighbour, Simon Sweeney, who had troubled Heaney as a child and who returns now to disturb him again. Sweeney appears in the poet's childhood as a transgressive figure, upon whom the child projects his fears of the alien and the unknown. Sweeney tells him:

> When they bade you listen
> in the bedroom dark
> to wind and rain in the trees
> and think of tinkers camped
> under a heeled-up cart
>
> you shut your eyes and saw
> a wet axle and spokes
> in moonlight, and me
> streaming from the shower,
> headed for your door.
>
> (*SI* 62)

The specific nature of Sweeney's deviance, which marks him as an alien and transgressive presence, is registered by the poet when he first recognizes his old neighbour. 'I know you, Simon Sweeney,' he says, 'for an old Sabbath-breaker | who has been dead for years' (*SI* 61). Sweeney stands outside the community because he transgresses its Christian injunction against working on Sunday –

the Sabbath Day, traditionally dedicated to rest and religious contemplation. Sweeney's response to the poet's remembered piety has a double force to it, as he tells the poet 'Damn all you know'. On the one hand, Sweeney is condemning Heaney for his presumptuousness, indicating that, in his uninformed ignorance, he knows nothing ('damn all'). On the other hand, his riposte runs deeper than this, as he also condemns (damns) all of the knowledge, all of the traditional pieties, that the poet had passively half-accepted for so many years. In an interview published three years before *Station Island* appeared, Heaney had mapped out this semi-detached position in the following terms:

> I'm not what you'd call a pious Catholic, I don't go to Mass much, and the doctrines of the Faith aren't my constant reading . . . but I guess it was part of the texture of growing up. I was going to Confession into my twenties, and the whole of my life was permeated with it. I've never felt any need to rebel or do a casting-off of God or anything like that, because I think in this day anthropologists and mythologists have taught us a lot, to live with our myths.[14]

Sweeney provides the first signal of an interrogation of Heaney's religious sense of self which runs through the poem as a whole and which finds focus again in section IV, where the poet encounters another neighbour, Terry Keenan. Keenan had joined the priesthood as an adolescent and served on the missions in South America, proselytising for the Roman Catholic faith. He died when his health was broken by the alien climate and conditions. The poet, in addressing Keenan, sees his priestly vocation as a futile surrender to convention, with the young man 'doomed to the decent thing' (*SI* 70). In the poet's eyes, Keenan is virtually sacrificed to the common pieties of his community:

> Something in them would be ratified
> when they saw you at the door in your black suit,
> arriving like some sort of holy mascot.

> You gave too much relief, you raised a siege
> the world had laid against their kitchen grottoes
> hung with holy pictures.

But, again, like Simon Sweeney, Keenan responds forcefully to the poet's easy self-assurance and turns to interrogating the poet's own sense of self. 'What are you doing, going through these motions?' he asks, 'Unless you are here taking the last look' (*SI* 71). Keenan's question penetrates to the heart of 'Station Island' and he effectively queries what the nature and purpose of Heaney's pilgrimage are. As Neil Corcoran has observed, what the poem presents us with is a peculiarly ironic, even reversed, form of pilgrimage, which 'leads to no confirmation in the religion and values of the tribe, but to something very like a renunciation of them'.[15]

The issue of Heaney's relationship to his sense of religous faith is brought to a head in section XI of the poem, when Heaney recalls another local priest, who had returned to the North from Spain and who, administering confession to Heaney, had once set him the penance of translating into English 'something by Juan de la Cruz' (*SI* 89) – the Spanish mystic, St John of the Cross. Heaney offers his translation as the balance of section XI of the poem. The prayer translated is a profession of faith in religious conviction, in the face of a crisis of belief. Faith is figured in the poem as an 'eternal fountain' which 'call[s] out to every creature' (*SI* 90). The prayer insists throughout on the validity of such beautiful and pure images of faith, despite the fact that the writer is, at the time of writing, uncertain of his beliefs. His crisis is insistently registered by the refrain which completes each stanza with the phrase 'although it is the night'. In the context of the other interrogations of religious belief which we find taking place in 'Station Island', we might feel that, in being imported into Heaney's poem, what happens to St John's prayer is that the balance of the individual stanzas shifts from the profession of faith to the confession of crisis. Within this context, the prayer seems less an articulation of consolation than an acknowledgement of a certain failure of belief.

This same reaction to orthodox religious doctrine can be discerned elsewhere in *Station Island*, especially in a poem such as 'In Illo Tempore', where Heaney again recalls his experiences of religion in childhood. Remembering his attendance at church services, he recollects how 'The big missal splayed | and dangled silky ribbons | of emerald and purple and watery white' (*SI* 118). This leads him on to recall the passive, unquestioning attitude which religion inculcated in the community, as he observes: 'Intransitively we would assist, | confess, receive. The verbs | assumed us. We adored.' This religion leaves no room for independence of thought or action.

We have been tracing Heaney's questioning of traditional religious orthodoxies through from the opening section of 'Station Island'. The second poem in the sequence sets in train another line of interrogation, already familiar to us from our consideration of *Field Work*. In this section, Heaney encounters the nineteenth-century Irish writer William Carleton, who published his own account of the Station Island ritual as *The Lough Derg Pilgrim*. Carleton renounced Catholicism and denounced the pilgrimage tradition as an act of unthinking superstition. As he appears in the poem, he is fully aware of the political implications of rejecting his Catholic identity and deriding it in print:

> hard-mouthed Ribbonmen and Orange bigots
> made me into the old fork-tongued turncoat
> who mucked the byre of their politics.
>
> If times were hard, I could be hard too.
> I made the traitor in me sink the knife.

> (*SI* 65)

It is his distaste for stagnant political orthodoxies of all kinds, whether Catholic (in the form of the militant 'Ribbonmen') or Protestant (the 'Orange bigots'), that leads Carleton to reject the pieties of his own community. His hard-edged self-positioning prompts Heaney to attempt to justify what we have already noted as his own habitual political ambiguities. He explains to Carleton that the militancy that he (Carleton) had grown up with had declined, in the community of Heaney's childhood, to the meaningless formalism of an empty subservient and pietistic nationalism:

> 'I have no mettle for the angry role,'
> I said. 'I come from County Derry,
> born in earshot of an Hibernian hall
>
> where a band of Ribbonmen played hymns to Mary.
> By then the brotherhood was a frail procession
> staggering home drunk on Patrick's Day.[']

This compromised, complacent background notwithstanding, however, Heaney is forced in later sections of 'Station Island' to confront the justifications and consequences that violent political actions imply. In the middle segment of the poem he encounters three young men whose deaths have resulted from the political situation. One is his cousin, Colum McCartney, the significance of whose presence in the poem we have already considered; a second is William Strathern, another acquaintance who, like Sean Armstrong, was murdered by loyalist gunmen in a random sectarian killing. Much in the manner of 'A Postcard from North Antrim', Heaney imagines the immediate particulars of Strathern's life – lying in bed beside his wife – as the killers arrive at his door. As he had done in his encounter with Carleton, Heaney finds himself attempting to justify his own political and poetic ambiguities to Strathern: ' "Forgive the way I have lived indifferent – I forgive my timid circumspect involvement," I I I surprised myself by saying' (*SI* 80). Strathern's response is direct and chilling: ' "Forgive I my eye," he said, "That's all above my head." ' ' Like Armstrong, Strathern had been shot in the head by his killers, so that his riposte to Heaney not only dismisses the poet's attempt in some measure to justify himself, but, in fact, brings that gesture of self-justification into confrontation with the brutal reality of his own violent death.

What Heaney demonstrates throughout 'Station Island' is that there are no simple ways of engaging with the Northern Irish situation. This point is underlined by his imagined encounter in the poem with a third young man whose death was connected with the political situation. In section IX, the poet believes he hears the voice of a prisoner who starved himself to death in jail. It is likely that Heaney has in mind here Francis Hughes, a Bellaghy neighbour who was imprisoned for IRA activities and who took part in the hunger strikes of 1980–1, when republican prisoners refused food in protest over the government's decision to reclassify them as 'criminals' rather than as 'political prisoners'. In all, ten men lost their lives; Hughes was the second of the group to die. In *The Redress of Poetry*, Heaney writes of his discomfort at the fact that he, ironically, was staying in the Oxford University rooms of a serving government minister on the night that Hughes died:

> It was a classic moment of conflicting recognitions, self-division, inner quarrel, a moment of dumbness and inadequacy when it felt like a betrayal to be enjoying the hospitality of an Establishment college and occupying, if only accidentally, the room of a British minister. (*RP* 188)

In the same piece, he also discusses the bind in which he felt he – in common with most other constitutional nationalists – was placed by the hunger strikes:

> As the Thatcher administration remained unmoved in the face of the deaths, and the cortèges kept winding from the prison gates to the local graves, there began to be something almost unseemly about the scruple which prevented a show of support for the hunger strikers' immediate claims – a support withheld because logically it would have been taken as an endorsement of the violent means and programmes of the Provisional IRA. Such caution had produced only silence, and now the silence was by default appearing like assent to the triumphalist, implacable handling of the affair by the Thatcher cabinet. (*RP* 187)

What we find in section IX of 'Station Island', then, is a sense of the poet's responsibility to act in some way in the face of this complex and depressing situation. The issue which lay at the centre of the hunger strikes dispute has a particular force for Heaney, in that, in seeking to criminalize republican (and loyalist) prisoners, the government was denying that their actions were politically motivated and had been undertaken as a response to the political crisis. This raises for Heaney, again, the question of what kind of response to the situation is appropriate and adequate. Though he does not condone Hughes's violent actions, he nevertheless recognizes them as one kind of response to the contemporary crisis (a recognition refused by the government). This prompts him once again to call himself to task for the inadequacy of his own response, as he cries: 'I repent I My unweaned life that kept me competent I To sleepwalk with connivance and mistrust' and 'I hate how quick I was to know my place. I I hate where I was born, hate everything I That made me biddable and unforthcoming' (*SI* 85).

It is, finally, the figure of James Joyce who releases Heaney from this sense of failed responsibility and inadequate responsiveness which surfaces again and again in 'Station Island'. It is Joyce's hand which 'stretche[s] down from the jetty' (*SI* 92) in the final section of the poem, as Heaney returns to the mainland at the end of his pilgrimage. Joyce, the *émigré* writer who left Ireland for Paris, dismisses Heaney's 'peasant pilgrimage' as an irrelevant waste of time and has little patience for his sense of inadequacy and penitence: 'don't be so earnest,' he cautions him, 'let others wear the sackcloth and the ashes' (*SI* 93). Joyce sets out for Heaney a programme for proceeding in his career as a poet, exhorting him to 'Cultivate a work-lust' and telling him that 'The main thing is to write | for the joy of it' – as Joyce himself did in playfully dismantling and refashioning the English language itself in *Finnegans Wake*. He further advises Heaney:

> Keep at a tangent.
> When they make the circle wide, it's time to swim
>
> out on your own and fill the element
> with signatures on your own frequency,
> echo soundings, searches, probes, allurements,
>
> elver-gleams in the dark of the whole sea.

(*SI* 93–4)

Heaney's Joyce here proposes a view of literature which detaches it from the necessity to provide a direct engagement with the particularities of the immediate political situation. In one sense, this might well be interpreted as a kind of 'cop out' on Heaney's part. If critics like Fennell, Carson, and Lloyd call Heaney to task for failing adequately to respond to the immediate political moment (and if Heaney himself, in some measure, seems to agree with this critique), this closing section of 'Station Island' might well be taken as Heaney's abandonment of the political in the face of his own failure. Such a view of the situation would not be entirely unjustified. Looking back over the span of Heaney's poems on the Irish crisis, we might feel that the poet seems finally to offer us little enough by way of a productive engagement with that crisis. When Heaney published *Station Island* a decade on from his fanciful image of reconciliation in 'Funeral Rites', the list of the dead had increased, as had the sense of bitterness and rancour on all sides in the dispute. Likewise, Heaney's learned disquisitions on Viking lore, archaeology, and etymology have always seemed terribly esoteric and far removed from the lives of those who have borne most in the conflict – the working-class families in Ireland and Britain from whom the majority of the combatants (republican and loyalist militants, British soldiers) and casualties are drawn. We might also say that Heaney's poems about bog-recovered bodies received a grim and bitter echo in 1999, when the IRA provided details of where it had buried the bodies of several catholics it had murdered, with the result that a number of extensive excavations were undertaken – most of them failing to yield any remains. This being said, however, it must also be noted that what characterizes Heaney's poems on the political situation is a deep sense of honest striving towards some kind of meaningful encounter with the history and politics of his native country. If he does fail in this attempt, perhaps that failure is more a testament to the complexity of the situation than to his attempts to bend his poetic responsibility towards it. Heaney is one of a large number of writers who turned their attention to the subject of Northern Ireland. Much of this writing has been glibly and ignorantly exploitative of the conflict; Heaney ranks as one of a handful of writers who have genuinely struggled to bring their work into some kind of fruitful relationship with the contemporary political situation and its historical antecedants.

Joyce's advice to Heaney to turn away from immediate political concerns would appear to be confirmed by a later poem in *Station Island* – 'The Old Icons' – in which Heaney appears finally to disengage himself from the kind of traditional nationalist orthodoxies and pieties to which he had, for much of his life, pledged a kind of wavering allegiance. We should note, however, that the turn away from Irish politics does not signal the advent of an apolitical Heaney. If anything, it indicates a broadening of his political canvas. From *Station Island* onwards, Heaney's political concerns become more wide-ranging, as evidenced by the inclusion of poems such as 'From the Land of the Unspoken' and 'From the Republic of Conscience' in *The Haw Lantern* (the latter poem having been first published as an Amnesty International pamphlet on Human Rights Day in 1985). This broadening of political interest is also registered in the amount of space dedicated to poets from Eastern Europe in *The Government of the Tongue*. Indeed Neil Corcoran has very usefully observed that while 'the island of Ireland and the configuration of Northern Ireland seem within hailing distance' of the 'political and topographical nowheres'[16] of some of the parabolic poems included in *The Haw Lantern*, taken as a whole these intricate allegorical poems 'sound so unrecognizably different from earlier Heaney styles as to appear almost like translations from another language'. Corcoran sees the adoption of a dislocated, phantasmal geography, inflected by eastern European concerns as affording Heaney 'a kind of mask, persona or alternative self, an alibi or alias' – something we will also see him find in the focal character of the medieval Irish poem, *Buile Suibhne*. For Corcoran, the effect of this is that 'the lyric becomes what it has never been in Heaney's work before: abstract, diagnostic, analytic, dispassionate, admonitory, forensic, post-mortem'.[17] Helen Vendler has described *The Haw Lantern* as 'Heaney's first book of the virtual' and in Heaney's later work it is precisely the territory of the virtual – where the real and the imagined map onto each other – that begins increasingly to concern him.[18]

4

'It was marvellous and actual': Familiarity and Fantasy

Seamus Heaney once noted in an interview that, sometime after *North* was published, he wrote to the playwright Brian Friel, observing of his poetic practice that he 'no longer wanted a door into the dark'. 'I wanted a door into the light,' he observed, 'to be able to use the first person singular to mean *me* and my lifetime.'[1] In the previous chapter we dwelt almost exclusively on the politically informed poetry which Heaney continued to write after *North*, but we should note that, from *Field Work* onwards, Heaney does begin to reintroduce into his work a kind of poetry that is less immediately political, a poetry more rooted in the world of personal concerns. Indeed, viewed in this light, we can see *Field Work* itself as falling very roughly into two halves. In the first stretch of the collection, Heaney continues to struggle with public themes, pursuing further the debates which he initiated in *North*, but, in the second, he turns to contemplate more intimate, more personal concerns.

In part this transition between the two halves of the volume (and, we might say, between the middle phase of Heaney's career and his later departures) is mediated through the sequence of poems that lies at the heart of *Field Work* – the 'Glanmore Sonnets'. We have already seen the significance of Glanmore for Heaney in our examination of *North*'s 'Exposure'. In that poem, Glanmore serves as a site of conflict. On the one hand, Heaney's removal to the rural south of Ireland, far distant from the day-to-day experience of the Northern troubles, prompts him to re-evaluate the exact nature of his political commitments as a poet. But, on the other hand, it also provokes a certain sense of anxiety and guilt about his abandonment of his home territory in a time of political crisis. In the 'Glanmore Sonnets', by contrast, Heaney celebrates his family's stint of living in County Wicklow with a kind of ease and freedom that 'Exposure' signally lacks.

In part this celebration marks something of a return for Heaney to the concerns of his early poetry, in which he sought an easy engagement with the particulars of the immediate, natural world. We might note, indeed, that the sonnet sequence opens with several images which will be familiar to us from Heaney's earliest work. The first and second of the Glanmore poems offer the task of ploughing as an image of the poetic act. '[A]rt', he tells us in sonnet I, could be 'a paradigm of earth new from the lathe I Of ploughs' (FW 33) and, in sonnet II, he recurs to the image we first saw him deploy in *Death of a Naturalist's* 'Follower', when he sees the act of turning lines of verse as being analogous to the turning of the plough from one furrow into another: 'Vowels ploughed into other, opened ground, I Each verse returning like the plough turned round' (FW 34).

In addition to deploying an imagery which echoes that of his earliest work, Heaney also offers here a sense of the nature of the poetic act which has much in common with his earlier sense of poetry. In sonnet II, he compares the poet's work to that of the sculptor, as, much in the manner of such early poems as 'The Diviner', 'The Forge', and 'Thatcher', he sees both figures as artisans who seek to draw from their mundane raw material an aesthetic form which lies naturally within it:

> 'These things are not secrets but mysteries,'
> Oisin Kelly told me years ago
> In Belfast, hankering after stone
> That connived with the chisel, as if the grain
> Remembered what the mallet tapped to know.

Throughout the 'Glanmore Sonnets' Heaney closely engages once more with the particulars of his immediate surroundings, seeking significances within them, just as his friend Oisin Kelly has sought the contours of his finished sculpture within the block of raw stone he worked upon. In sonnet III, Heaney finds the natural world offering a kind of poetry of its own to him, as he writes:

> This evening the cuckoo and the corncrake
> (So much, too much) consorted at twilight.
> It was all crepuscular and iambic.

and

> Outside a rustling and twig-combing breeze
> Refreshes and relents. Is cadences.

(FW 35)

In each case, the world around the poet organizes itself into natural poetic rhythms – 'iambs' and 'cadences'.

In the seventh poem in the sequence, Heaney once again finds himself drawn to the particularities of place-names, as he recalls those names included as a kind of ritual in the gale-warnings routinely broadcast on the radio: 'Dogger, Rockall, Malin, Irish Sea' and 'Minches, Cromarty, The Faroes' (FW 39). One particular gale drives a group of French trawlers into a nearby Wicklow harbour and Heaney savours 'their bright names': 'L'Etoile, Le Guillemot, La Belle Hélène'. The unexpected sight of these exotic, foreign intrusions into the world of the local and the quotidian prompts the poet to an observation which will prove central to much of his poetry in this phase of his career. 'It was marvellous I And actual', he writes, stressing in equal measure the wondrous quality of the experience and its concreteness – the experience is at one and the same time extraordinary and firmly rooted in the material world (their exotic names notwithstanding, these are not the mythical longboats that we find arising out of a Viking past in Heaney's earlier poetry, but rather ordinary French fishing vessels).

We will return to Heaney's sense of the relationship between the marvellous and the actual later in this chapter. But, first, we might note that, just as he celebrates the actual as providing a kind of access to the marvellous, so too, in the 'Glanmore Sonnets', he celebrates the deep significance of the domestic and the intimate. The figure of the poet's wife is several times invoked in these poems. In sonnet III, she appears in order to puncture his inflated sense of his own life as a poet. In eulogizing their rural existence, he begins to draw a parallel between their lives in Glanmore and Dorothy and William Wordsworth's life together in 'Dove Cottage' in Grasmere, in the English Lake District. His wife, refusing the connection, cuts across him: 'She interrupts: I "You're not going to compare us two . . ." ' Later in the volume, in 'An Afterwards', she again performs the same deflationary role, when Heaney imagines her as a kind of female Dante, encountering him on her rounds of the Inferno. Telling him that she has 'closed [her] widowed ears | To the sulphurous news of poets and poetry' (*FW* 44), she offers, in the closing lines of the poem, a slyly humourous assessment of her husband's life:

> 'You weren't the worst. You aspired to a kind,
> Indifferent, faults-on-both-sides tact.
> You left us first, and then those books, behind.'

Elsewhere in the 'Glanmore Sonnets', the poet's wife serves as a point of intimate, human contact which offers a bulwark against terror and anguish. In sonnet VIII, the poet's mind fills with images of the aftermath of bloody conflict – 'I thought of dew on armour and carrion. | What would I meet, bloodboltered, on the road?' (*FW* 40) – and with unspecified fears of the kind he once registered in a poem such as 'The Barn' – 'How deep into the woodpile sat the toad? | What welters through this dark hush on the crops?' The poem then shifts to an image of an old woman, comforting a Down's Syndrome child, a shared memory of a trip made with his wife. In the closing couplet of the poem, the poet turns to his spouse, urgently seeking sexual relief from these accumulated fears and anxieties: 'Come to me quick, I am upstairs shaking. | My all of you birchwood in lightning.'

In our analysis of *Death of a Naturalist*, we noted the clutch of marriage poems which Heaney includes in the closing section of his first collection. *Field Work* includes a similar group, not so much of marriage poems, as of poems concerning sexual intimacy. The 'Glanmore Sonnets' end, for instance, with a delicate evocation of the first sexual encounter between the poet and his wife. The context of the recollection is a dream in which he imagines the two of them as a pair of eloping lovers, in the manner of *The Merchant of Venice*'s Lorenzo and Jessica, or Diarmuid and Grainne from the traditional Irish story *Toríacht Diarmuida agus Grainne*. Switching from the mythical to the remembered, he writes:

> And in that dream I dreamt – how like you this? –
> Our first night years ago in that hotel
> When you came with your deliberate kiss
> To raise us towards that lovely and painful
> Covenants of flesh; our separateness;
> The respite in our dewy dreaming faces.

> (*FW* 42)

76

As so often in Heaney, the poem offers us a point of reference derived from the English Renaissance. The line 'how like you this?' is taken from Sir Thomas Wyatt's poem 'They fle from me that sometyme did me seke', in which the poet's lover, coming to him in the night and letting 'her lose gowne from her shoulders . . . fall', asks him 'dere hert, howe like you this?'[2] In Wyatt's poem, this sexual encounter is remembered with a certain degree of bitterness, as an instance of the pleasure now being denied him in his isolation, since 'all is torned . . . I Into a straunge fasshion for forsaking'. In Heaney's poem, by contrast, the moment of bold intimacy is presented, not as an episode recollected from a lost world, but, rather, in a complex sense, as a point of initiation. It is both a sexual initiation (a kind of 'initiation rite') and also the initiation into their lives together as partners.

The persistence of a certain kind of quiet longing and sexual intimacy is registered elsewhere in *Field Work* also, especially in such poems as 'The Otter', 'The Skunk', and sections of the title poem, 'Field Work', itself. In these poems Heaney offers tender images of a life of shared physical intimacies. Sometimes, as in 'The Skunk', these images are charged with a certain kind of comic incongruity, as the poet compares his wife – in her 'head-down, tail-up hunt in a bottom drawer I For the black plunge-line nightdress' (*FW* 48) – to a skunk he once saw in California. The humour of the comparison, in contrast with the raw sexual desire of a poem such as the eighth Glanmore sonnet, indicates the easy intimacy of a long-term, settled relationship.

The engagement with the intimate, the domestic, and the familial, which Heaney re-initiates in *Field Work*, continues in its successor volume, *Station Island*. In 'The Underground', the opening poem of the collection, Heaney again recollects the earliest days of his marriage, as he recalls a trip to a Proms concert at London's Albert Hall during his honeymoon. Heaney's children also appear at several points in this volume, with the poet explicitly dedicating two poems to them – 'A Hazel Stick for Catherine Ann' and 'A Kite for Michael and Christopher'. What the poems in which the children appear seem to offer is, again, a kind of initiation process, except that, now, it is the poet's offspring who are being initiated into the world of resonant particularities – the world from which much of Heaney's poetry is derived. In 'Changes' the poet leads one of his children to an old pump (an image always charged with heavy significance in Heaney's work) and they share together the unexpected pleasure of discovering a bird and her egg nestled in its disused spout. In closing, the poet exhorts his child to

> 'Remember this.
> It will be good for you to retrace this path
> when you have grown away and stand at last
> at the very centre of the empty city.'

(*SI* 37)

The gesture is strikingly reminiscent of numerous moments in another poet much concerned with childhood, William Wordsworth, especially his observation in 'Tintern Abbey' that the 'beauteous forms' which he has experienced in the countryside near the abbey have often come back to him 'in lonely rooms, and 'mid the din I Of towns and cities', affording him

> sensations sweet,
> Felt in the blood, and felt along the heart;
> And passing even into my purer mind,
> With tranquil restoration.[3]

What both Wordsworth and Heaney suggest is that what the rural experience, the intimate contact with nature, provides is a resource which can be drawn upon in other times and other circumstances.

In the two poems specifically titled for Heaney's children, we find, again, attention afforded to a particular object or experience which indicates significances beyond its immediate import. 'A Hazel Stick for Catherine Ann' memorializes a simple object – a hazel wand cut for the child by her father. In the child's hands, however, the stick is turned to a variety of uses. The imagination which plays upon the stick is emblematized by the glow-worm, which the child encounters for the first time ever on the same evening as her father trims the wand for her. In the closing lines of the poem, the insect and the stick are brought together, as the glow-worm's light brightens 'the eye I in the blunt cut end' of the stick (*SI* 43). What the stick gives access to, we might say, is a world of vision and illumination. 'A Kite for Michael and Christopher' traces a similar trajectory. The soaring of the kite seems to indicate a kind of transcendence of the material world. The poem closes on an unexpected note, however, as the poet signals to his children just what connection the kite affords:

> take it in your two hands, boys, and feel
> the strumming, rooted, long-tailed pull of grief.
> You were born fit for it.
> Stand in here in front of me
> and take the strain.

> (SI 44)

What the soaring kite offers is not an escape from the world, but a profound connection with the anguish of life – the 'long-tailed pull of grief'. That the poet should summon his children to experience this connection is indicative of the capacity of the kite to mediate the encounter, to make it possible for them to 'take the strain'. The kite provides, thus, not a point of exit from the world of 'gravity', but a point of fruitful and meaningful engagement with that world.

What Heaney sets out in 'A Kite for Michael and Christopher' is, as much as anything else, an aesthetic or poetic creed, and we can see the kite as a figure for the creative act. We will notice that a common thread links a poem such as 'Glanmore Sonnets' VII, where the actual and the marvellous are deeply intertwined, and 'A Kite for Michael and Christopher', where the marvellous (in the form of the soaring kite) facilitates a productive encountering of the actual. Before we turn to explore the implications of these ideas for the general thrust of Heaney's later poetry, we might first consider a further set of poems in which Heaney again engages with the domestic and the familial. These are the poems in *The Haw Lantern* and *Seeing Things*, where Heaney attempts to come to terms with his relationship with his parents.

Heaney's mother died in the autumn of 1984, his father two years later. *The Haw Lantern* was the first collection of Heaney's to appear in the wake of these deaths and it is in many respects permeated by a sense of loss and absence. Absence itself is precisely the theme of sonnet 8 of the 'Clearances' sequence of the volume, which opens with the lines

> I thought of walking round and round a space
> Utterly empty, utterly a source

> Where the decked chestnut tree had lost its place
> In our front hedge above the wallflowers.
>
> (*HL* 32)

Later in the poem, Heaney characterizes the tree as his 'coeval chestnut' and the biographical reference is glossed in *The Government of the Tongue*, where he explains that the tree had been planted in the year of his birth, but that it was cut down after the Heaneys moved house, when he was a teenager. Later in life Heaney comes to meditate on the tangible empty space that the tree had occupied:

> I began to think of the space where the tree had been. In my mind's eye I saw it as a kind of luminous emptiness, a warp and waver of light, and once again, a way that I find hard to define, I began to identify with that space just as years before I had identified with the young tree. (*GT* 3–4)

In Heaney's poetic vision this space marked by absence 'become[s] a bright nowhere' (*HL* 32) – a site of loss which is also a point of luminescence. In this sense, Heaney attempts both to register loss and to reimagine it as something potentially productive.

Elsewhere in 'Clearances' Heaney endeavours to encounter directly the reality of the loss of his parents. In the second poem of the sequence he offers a slightly whimsical image of his mother's afterlife, as she arrives back after her death to a kind of celestial version of her own parental home. Her dead father welcomes her 'With spectacles pushed back on a clean bald head' (*HL* 26) and she re-enters a familiar meticulous and precise world: 'The kettle whistled. Sandwich and teascone | Were present and correct.' The attention to detail here, somewhat comic in the context of traditional notions of the afterlife, is characteristic of the sequence as a whole. Indeed, it is only through an engagement with the details of a common – in the sense both of 'shared' and of 'everyday' – life that Heaney is able to come to terms with his mother's death. What he recalls of his life with his mother – and what enables him to reconcile himself to her passing – is a series of concrete tasks which they shared together. In the third poem in the sequence, for instance, he recollects times he spent with her on Sunday mornings peeling potatoes, while the rest of the family were at church. This simple task constitutes for Heaney a kind of intimacy which has a significance far outstripping surface appearances. Indeed, it is the image of this unspoken intimacy which returns to the poet's mind and consoles him far more than prayer does at the point of his mother's death. While the priest, he tells us, was intoning the prayers for the dying,

> And some were responding and some crying
> I remembered her head bent towards my head,
> Her breath in mine, our fluent dipping knives –
> Never closer the whole rest of our lives.

(HL 27)

We are offered an image of a similar kind of intimacy in the fifth poem in the sequence, where Heaney remembers performing another domestic chore with his mother – folding sheets together as they took them off the clothes line. Again, the routine, formal rhythms of the task provide a kind of structure within which their unspoken and unacknowledged connection can find a place:

> ... we'd stretch and fold and end up hand to hand
> For a split second as if nothing had happened
> For nothing had that had not always happened
> Beforehand, day by day, just touch and go,
> Coming close again by holding back.

(HL 29)

The poem speaks both of a failure of true intimacy, a stultifying lack of real communication, and also of the way in which such communication can be (and must be) channelled into alternative modes of expression. The faint touchings of the customary routine of the domestic chore become a means whereby mother and son can make contact – however fleeting – with each other.

In the fourth of the 'Clearances' poems, Heaney returns to a topic which was a significant concern of his in *Death of a Naturalist*: the sense of alienation from his family that he felt as he had grown away from them educationally and culturally. In 'Clearances' he registers how, with his mother, he effected a kind of compromise, in an attempt to bridge the gap between them. In her company, he tells us, he would change his way of speaking, switching from his acquired, educated register to the

manner of speech which was native to him: 'I'd *naw* and *aye* |
And decently relapse into the wrong | Grammar' (*HL* 28). The
effect of the compromise is to keep mother and son 'allied and
at bay' and, again, we get a sense of a balance being struck
between a certain failure of communication, on the one hand,
and the effecting of that communication through alternative
channels, on the other.

If Heaney manages to come to terms with his relationship
with his mother in *Haw Lantern*'s 'Clearances', in *Seeing Things*
he attempts to work through his relationship with his father –
a relationship which, we will recall from a poem such as *Death
of a Naturalist*'s 'Follower', is altogether more vexed. In 'Man
and Boy' the poet effects a connection with his father by tele-
scoping three generations of fathers and sons. His access to his
own father's death is ventured through his father's experience
of *his* father's death, as he ran through the fields to tell him
that the mower (with his scythe, a figure for death in the
poem) had finished his work. The poet combines this vision of
the past with a vision of the future, as he imagines himself
in old age piggybacked 'Like a witless elder rescued from the
fire' (*ST* 15). Heaney is alluding here to the story of Virgil's
Aeneid, in which Aeneas carries his father Anchises from the
ruins of Troy, following the fall of the city. In Heaney's version
of the filial myth, however, it is he himself as son turned old
man who will be carried away, not by one of his own sons, but
rather by a youthful incarnation of his father. What we get here,
then, is a collapsing of male generations into a kind of equiva-
lence, as a relationship of equality, interchangeability, and
continuity is established among the various fathers and sons
who figure in the poem (and this, we might say, serves as a
contrast to the ordered sequence of male generations presented
in 'Digging').

A similar resolution to the generational struggle between
fathers and sons is effected in a further pair of poems in *Seeing
Things*: 'The Ash Plant' and the immediately succeeding 'I.I.87'.
In the first of these poems, Heaney offers a picture of his father
in his last days, lying in bed, inactive, the world continuing
with its routines without him. As his father dies away from the
world, one last spark of habit prompts him to reach out for his
'ash plant' – the stick which he regularly carried about with him

on his rounds of the family farm. The action of connecting with the stick has the effect of steadying the dying man and affording him a sense of location:

> his wasting hand
> Gropes desperately and finds the phantom limb
> Of an ash plant in his grasp, which steadies him.
> Now he has found his touch he can stand his ground.

(*ST* 19)

In the short, three-line poem which immediately follows 'The Ash Plant', Heaney extends the connection from his father to himself:

> Dangerous pavements.
> But I face the ice this year
> With my father's stick.

(*ST* 20)

Now that his father is dead, he has acquired as an inheritance his father's stick, and he too feels steadied and located with it in his possession. The conflicts which he experienced with his father have been dissolved by his parent's death and he is able to come to terms both with the death itself and with the psychological inheritance which his father has bequeathed to him through the symbolic possession of his father's stick. We might note a rather obvious psycho-sexual connection here, in that the acquisition of the phallic object of the stick may be emblematic, at a sexual level, of the final resolution of a kind of oedipal struggle between son and father. In more general terms, we can say that possessing this tangible marker of continuity with his lost parent serves to steady the poet within the uncertainties of his own life – the 'ice' which he must negotiate. Blake Morrison, who wrote the first book-length study of Heaney, delineates a similar symbolic moment of filial possession to Heaney's in his memoir of his own parent's death, *And When Did You Last See Your Father?* As he prepares for his father's funeral, he writes: 'I put on his white nylon shirt, black tie, grey suit, black woollen socks, black shoes. I am going to his funeral in his clothes' and, again, at the funeral itself: 'I stand in his clothes – how well they fit me now – gazing down at the earth. Snow blows across his black scuffed shoes, the bottom of his greatcoat, his trouser turn-ups.'[4]

The ash plant in these poems figures as a kind of symbolic object that provides access not to a realm which transcends the everyday material world, but rather to one which facilitates a productive engagement with that world. In the hand of the dying man, cut off from the realm of his customary routines, it offers a sense of connectedness and location; after his death, in the hands of his son, it offers a different sense of connectedness, allowing the son more easily to negotiate the uncertainties of the world he inhabits. In this sense, the ash plant has much in common with the various other symbolic objects and routines we have encountered in much of Heaney's later poetry – the hazel stick and the kite we find in the poems written for his children, for instance, or the rigidly choreographed routine of the domestic chores we encounter in 'Clearances', or even the trawlers of 'Glanmore Sonnets' VII, which prompt Heaney to forge a connection between the 'marvellous' and the 'actual'.

The complex relationship which is posited in these poems between the 'marvellous' and the 'actual', or, as we might re-phrase it, between the transcendent and the material, is entirely characteristic of the poetic thrust of much of Heaney's later work. Traditionally, poetry is seen as providing access to a realm which transcends the immediate world of everyday life. It is this quality of poetry which Sir Philip Sidney indicates when he writes in his sixteenth-century *Defence of Poetry* of the capacity of the writer to deliver a 'golden world', where nature itself can only deliver a world of brass. In the twentieth century, this traditional orthodoxy has increasingly been subject to interrogation.

Heaney's relationship to the issues of transcendence and materiality is complex. In his earliest poems, we recall, he is profoundly invested in the project of providing a space, within his poems, for the particularities of his immediate, native world. He is inspired in this by his perception of Patrick Kavanagh's poetic project, excited by the prospect of rendering into print what he calls 'the unregarded data of the usual life' (*GT* 7). In such a rendering, the particular comes to assume a more resonant significance, and, in this sense, the transcendent is predicated upon a close engagement with the particular. In Sidney's terms, we might say that the golden world is achieved not by a kind of alchemical transformation of the base metal of the natural world, but rather by focusing on the natural world a poetic eye for detail so acute that it can bring to perception the hitherto unobserved gold within the compound of the everyday. Neil Corcoran anatomizes this position very neatly by quoting a maxim of the French poet Phillippe Jaccottet (who he arrives at via the Irish poet Derek Mahon): "'Il y a une autre réalité mais elle est en celle-ci", "There is another reality, but it is in this one"'.[5]

An engagement with the relationship between the material or the particular, on the one hand, and the transcendent, on the other, remains a constant concern throughout Heaney's career. In his later poems, however, we can see Heaney beginning to offer a somewhat more complex sense of the nature of the interface between the material and the transcendent. Here, Heaney, even as he maintains a certain belief in the possibility of transcendence, at the same time maintains a certain sceptical attitude towards that possibility. We can see this balance between faith and scepticism sketched out in a poem such as 'The King of the Ditchbacks' from *Station Island*. The poem is concerned with the process of translation, specifically, with Heaney's own attempts to translate the medieval Irish poem *Buile Suibhne* into English. *Buile Suibhne* is an extremely important work to Heaney (as it has been to a number of other Irish writers – Flann O'Brien incorporated sections of his own translation of the poem into his novel *At Swim-Two-Birds*) and references to the work recur throughout his later poetry. Many people have commented on the rhyming echo between the names 'Sweeney' and 'Heaney' and have seen Sweeney as a kind of poetic alter ego for Heaney himself.[6]

The poem tells the story of an Irish king, Sweeney, who, following an altercation with the Christian priest, Ronan, is cursed by the priest so that he is transformed into a bird and goes mad. He then flies restlessly from tree to tree, wandering about Ireland, lamenting his plight in poetry. The story has several points of attraction for Heaney. On the one hand, Sweeney serves as a figure for the artist: 'displaced, guilty, assuaging himself by his utterance, it is possible to read the work as an aspect of the quarrel between free creative imagination and the constraints of religious, political, and domestic obligation' (*SA*, Introduction). On the other hand, Heaney's interest in the story is also prompted by the insight it offers into the anxieties occasioned by the collision of two cultural systems –

85

native Celtic paganism and the Christian culture which succeeded it. As Heaney himself observes: 'the literary imagination which fastened upon [Sweeney] as an image was clearly in the grip of a tension between the newly dominant Christian ethos and the older, recalcitrant Celtic temperament' (*SA*, Introduction).[7] In this sense, we might see Sweeney as a 'liminal', or threshold, figure, suspended between two worlds – the traditional Celtic world which pledges its faith to an immediate physical realm, and a religious world which offers fidelity to the non-material, the spiritual, the transcendent.

If we turn to 'King of the Ditchbacks' we can see how Sweeney's positioning between these two realms is consonant with Heaney's sense of the relation between the material and the transcendent. In the second section of the poem, Heaney writes of his sense of Sweeney's presence nearby as he was translating the Irish text: 'He was depending on me as I hung out on the limb of a translated phrase like a youngster dared out on to an alder branch over the whirlpool' (*SI* 57). The sentence is deceptive in its clarity and is densely compacted with meaning. Heaney feels himself to be 'out on a limb', taking risks in translating the poem. Sweeney, he tells us, is 'depending' on him. The word 'depending' has a double force here. On the one hand, it indicates the responsibility which the situation imposes on Heaney – Sweeney requires Heaney to translate his story so that his history can be articulated. On the other hand, 'depending' also means 'to hang down, be suspended'. One of the examples of this usage which the *Oxford English Dictionary* . offers is Southey's 'The mountain-ash ... depends its branches to the stream below'.[8] So we can see that, in a peculiar way, the text folds in on itself here. Sweeney is reliant on Heaney to tell his story. In this sense, Heaney is forced by his responsibility out onto the branch of creative risk. At the same time, however, Sweeney may also be seen as hanging on Heaney, as the branch Heaney ventures onto itself hangs 'over the whirlpool'. Sweeney is a kind of principle of gravity, pulling Heaney downwards, even as he is also a principle of inspiration, spurring Heaney on to creative effort. His position, then, is finely – and precariously – balanced between the two forces exerted upon him. Heaney himself has identified Yeats as an emblematic precursor in mediating between the opposing poles of such dichotomies:

Yeats was always passionately beating on the wall of the physical world in order to provoke an answer from the other side. His studies were arcane, his cosmology was fantastic and yet his intellect remained undeluded. Rational objectives were often rationally allowed by him, if only to be imaginatively and rhetorically overwhelmed. Yeats's embrace of the supernatural, in other words, was not at all naïve; he was as alive as Larkin to the demeaning realities of bodily decrepitude and the obliterating force of death, but he deliberately resisted the dominance of the material over the spiritual. (*RP* 149–50)

We can see this sense of precarious doubleness at play in the closing section of 'King of the Ditchbacks' also. Here the speaking voice in the poem – which had been the poet's own voice – becomes conflated (or perhaps, more accurately, confused) with a modern Sweeney. The speaker is brought into the woods with his head 'dressed . . . in a fishnet' with 'leafy twigs' plaited through the meshes 'so [his] vision was a bird's | at the heart of a thicket'. After a time, the speaker feels himself experiencing a transformation: 'And I saw myself | rising to move in that dissimulation, | | top-knotted, masked in sheaves, noting | the fall of birds' (*SI* 58). The key word to focus on here is 'dissimulation', which, like 'depending', has a double force in this context. On the one hand, 'dissimulation' means 'the action of . . . dissembling; concealment of what really is, under a feigned semblance of something different; feigning . . . '. So Heaney would appear to be indicating that the transformation experienced by the speaker is really no transformation at all – it is no more than an effect of the speaker's taking on the 'disguise' or 'costume' which is imposed upon him. On the other hand, if we search more closely through the meanings of the word 'dissimulation' – listening for the ring of what Helen Vendler calls 'Heaney's etymological tuning fork'[9] – we find the following alternative sense of the word: 'A fanciful name for a "company" or flock of small birds'.[10] Adopting this meaning of the word, the lines in question take on a quite different sense, since, in this instance, the lines indicate a literal and actual transformation – the speaker, having become a bird himself, sees himself rise to move as part of a company of birds.

This sense of doubleness, of affirming a certain faith in transcendence while at the same time retaining a sense of that

87

transcendence as possibly being no more than a delusion – or, alternatively, of affirming faith in transcendence in defiance of the knowledge that transcendence is, objectively, no more than a delusion – is central to Heaney's later poetry, particularly in his 1991 volume *Seeing Things*. The very title of this collection rests precisely upon this sense of doubleness, in that it simultaneously indicates poetry's power to *perceive* and to *deceive*. 'Field of Vision' is a good example of the way in which Heaney pursues this theme in *Seeing Things*. Again, the title of the poem has a double inflection. The poem is about a woman who sits in a wheelchair, staring fixedly out into the countryside. Heaney compares her sight to the sight one experiences looking beyond 'a well-braced gate' into a field. The 'field of vision' of the title can be either the full extent of what one sees, or it can be the particular literal field, bounded by hedges, that lies beyond the gate which bars the viewer's way. Or, again, 'vision' itself can have a deeper, more mystical sense – it can be a felt perception which is either real or imaginary, as, for instance, in the case of a religious vision. Standing at the gate, we are told, you could see

> Deeper into the country than you expected
> And discovered that the field behind the hedge
> Grew more distinctly strange as you kept standing
> Focused and drawn in by what barred the way.
>
> (*ST* 22)

Here, again, as in the case of poems such as 'The Ash Plant', 'I.I.87', or 'A Hazel Stick for Catherine Ann', it is a solid material object which facilitates a peculiar kind of 'access' to the immaterial. The barrier of the gate is, ironically, what enables the viewer to penetrate more clearly the strangeness of the space which lies beyond it. In this sense, the poet imagines for the viewer an experience not unlike that of looking at a perceptual illusion such as the three-dimensional illustration of a cube which, if stared at fixedly, oscillates between appearing to come out of the page in one of two opposing directions. What we see in our field of vision is, likewise, Heaney seems to be suggesting, a flickering between the material and the visionary: what he registers, discussing Wallace Stevens in *The Redress of Poetry*, as 'the imagination pressing back against the pressure of reality' (1).

What interests Heaney here is precisely the threshold experience – the experience of being situated between two different states or conditions. This is, of course, we will recall, one of the features of the Sweeney story which Heaney found attractive. We can trace Heaney's own biographical sense of liminality in a poem such as 'Terminus' from *The Haw Lantern*. 'I grew up in between' (*HL* 5), he writes, and, in marked contrast to the unambiguously rural milieu of *Death of a Naturalist*, he indicates how the modern industrial world cast its shadow over his country childhood:

> When I hoked there, I would find
> An acorn and a rusted bolt.
>
> If I lifted my eyes, a factory chimney
> And a dormant mountain.
>
> If I listened, an engine shunting
> And a trotting horse.
>
> (*HL* 4)

The notion of the liminal, of negotiating between one realm or state and another, is central to the vision of *Seeing Things*, as Heaney exhorts himself to 'Relocate the bedrock in the threshold' (*ST* 56). An entire section of the second half of the book is given over to a group of poems with the general title 'Crossings', in the opening piece of which Heaney finds himself 'in the middle of the road' (*ST* 83) – echoing the opening line of Dante's *Divine Comedy*, which Heaney directly quotes earlier in the volume (in 'The Schoolbag'): *'nel mezzo del cammin'* ('in the middle of the way'). Likewise, Heaney closes *Seeing Things* with a piece entitled 'The Crossing'. This poem is, in fact, a translation of a section of Canto III of the *Inferno*, which details the poet's encountering of Charon – the mythical boatman who carries the souls of the dead over the River Styx to the underworld. This translation balances exactly another translation set at the opening of the volume – a section of Virgil's *Aeneid*, in which Aeneas seeks to venture into the underworld to encounter his dead father. ·

In the *Inferno*, it is the poet, Dante himself, accompanied by another poet, Virgil, who can make the journey which no other mortal can survive. Only Dante can return from the other world of the dead to the living world of everyday life. In the *Aeneid*, the hero can only make his journey and return if he carries with him a symbolic object – 'a bough made of gold | And its leaves and pliable twigs are made of it too' (*ST* 3). In a sense, we might say, returning (anachronistically) to Sidney, that Aeneas' double journey is only possible if it is facilitated by a token derived from the 'golden world' of artifice; likewise the journey of Dante to and from the underworld is a journey which only he, as a poet, can make. Viewed in this light, the essential thrust of *Seeing Things* is to suggest that the function of poetry (or of art generally) is precisely to sustain the threshold between different realms – to hold open the possibility of a negotiation between such realms. As Heaney observes in *The Government of the Tongue*: 'Poetry is more a threshold than a path, one constantly approached and constantly departed from, at which the reader and writer undergo in their different ways the experience of being at the same time summoned and released' (*GT* 108). The fundamental point of poetry is not to effect an arrival but to facilitate the possibility of 'crossings' – a fruitful interrelation of, we might say, the worlds of possibility and materiality.

This sense of the possibility of maintaining a fruitful channel between the mundane and the marvellous is finely caught by Heaney in one of the most striking poems included in *Seeing Things* – viii in the 'Lightenings' section of the volume – dubbed by Helen Vendler 'the theory-poem of the volume'.[11] The poem offers us a fanciful anecdote from the Irish historical annals. As the monks at the abbey of Clonmacnoise are at prayer, a ship appears in the air above them. The ship is dragging its anchor, which becomes caught in the chapel's altar rail. A member of the crew of the ship climbs down the rope and tries unsuccessfully to release it. The abbot suggests that the monks must intervene to save the man's life:

> 'This man can't bear our life here and will drown,'
> The abbot said, 'unless we help him.' So
> They did, the freed ship sailed, and the man climbed back
> Out of the marvellous as he had known it.
>
> (*ST* 62)

What the poem suggests is that the marvellous and the actual are not divorced, antithetical realms, but rather that there is a consonance between the two. As Henry Hart has noted, like the American poet Marianne Moore, Heaney realizes that 'the

90

visionary and the real are symbiotic rather than exclusive'.[12] The quotidian world of the monks constitutes the marvellous for the sailor of the visionary ship, just as his world in turn, constitutes the marvellous for the monks themselves. What the poet offers, in Heaney's view, is a channel of negotiation between these two territories.

In noting the connection between the views of poetry put forward by Heaney and by Marianne Moore, Henry Hart reminds us of Moore's famously calling for a poetry which offers 'imaginary gardens with real toads in them'. Heaney's first published book concerns itself very much with 'real toads', with the particulars of his rural surroundings, the flora and fauna of country life. In pursuing a poetic of this kind, Heaney was, we have noted, being faithful to the values which he perceived in the poetry of Patrick Kavanagh – a poetry which celebrated 'the unregarded data of the usual life'. Heaney writes in *The Government of the Tongue* that in the 1960s he 'was still more susceptible to the pathos and familiarity of the matter of Kavanagh's poetry than . . . alert to the liberation and subversiveness of its manner' (*GT* 10). Later in life, Heaney developed a more complex sense of what Kavanagh was seeking to achieve in his work. He began to perceive a shift in Kavanagh's poetic practice between the first and second halves of his career. The early Kavanagh, Heaney proposes, 'is pervious to this world's spirit more than it is pervious to his spirit . . . the experienced physical reality of Monaghan life imposes itself upon the poet's consciousness so that he necessarily composes himself, his poetic identity and his poems in relation to that encircling horizon of given experience'. (*GT* 5) By contrast, he suggests, 'a definite change is perceptible' in Kavanagh's later poetry:

> We might say that now the world is more pervious to his vision than he is pervious to the world. When he writes about places now, they are luminous spaces within his mind. They have been evacuated of their status as background, as documentary geography, and exist instead as transfigured images, sites where the mind projects its own force. In this later poetry, place is included within the horizon of Kavanagh's mind rather than the other way around.

As John Wilson Foster notes: Kavanagh here 'is re-evaluated and found to have moved from a substantial, local and self-expressive poetry to a weightless, placeless self-mastery'.[13]

91

In writing about Kavanagh here Heaney is also, in a way, writing about himself. The early Heaney too is 'pervious to the world', seeking to be faithful to its particulars. In the later Heaney, as in the later Kavanagh (or, at least, in Heaney's perception of the later Kavanagh), world becomes pervious to mind, as the particular becomes less important than the realm to which it gives access – the territory upon which mind can play. But perhaps, finally, for Heaney what is important is not so much mind or world in and of itself, but rather the state of perviousness that brings them into interaction. What increasingly comes to interest Heaney in his later poems is no longer either the real toads or the imaginary gardens, but rather the process of bringing the two together and the interaction to which that conjunction gives rise.

5

'Ourselves again, free-willed again, not bad': The Unpartitioned Intellect

Peter McDonald has observed of *Seeing Things* that it 'represents [Heaney's] most sustained attempt to achieve imaginative lift-off into a kind of poetry less constrained by identities (Irish or otherwise) and more openly metaphysical in its concerns'.[1] While this is undoubtedly true, it is also the case that the volume which immediately followed *Seeing Things* – *The Spirit Level* (1996) – offered something like a spiralling back to a number of Heaney's traditional poetic themes and interests. This is not exactly a case of a Freudian 'return of the repressed', but it is nevertheless true, as Neil Corcoran has argued, that *The Spirit Level* relocates Heaney's work 'very vividly [in] those social, historical and political contingencies which it appeared a large part of the effort of *Seeing Things* to raise itself clear of'.[2]

The historical and political contingencies which Corcoran points to can vividly be seen re-emerging in a poem such as 'The Flight Path', where a figure out of Heaney's personal and political past irrupts into the scene of the poem. Section 4 of 'The Flight Path' is set in 1979 – the year Heaney had his first experience of teaching at Harvard. Having just flown from New York to Dublin, he is seated on a train bound for Belfast, enjoying the 'Plain, simple / Exhilaration at being back' (*SL* 24), when a 'grimfaced' figure enters the scene. The poet had once dreamed that this man – a childhood schoolfriend – had solicited his help in blowing up a customs post on the Irish border, attempting to draw him into a cosy friendly conspiracy of violent destruction. Once Heaney had parked the explosives-laden van, he simply needed to walk on down the road to another vehicle:

> and get in with – here
> Another schoolfriend's name, a wink and a smile,
> I'd know him all right, he'd be in a Ford
> And I'd be home in three hours' time, as safe
> As houses . . .
>
> (*SL* 24–25)

The episode of the proxy-bomb is no more than a dream, but on the journey to Belfast the grimfaced schoolfriend is a real presence, berating Heaney for his failure to write a clearly partisan poetry that registers a definite solidarity with his own community: 'When, for fuck's sake, are you going to write / Something for us?' (*SL* 25). This is precisely the impossible demand of the political activist that Heaney registers and rejects in *The Redress of Poetry*:

> For the activist, there is going to be no point in envisaging an order which is comprehensive of events but not in itself productive of new events. Engaged parties are not going to be grateful for a mere image – no matter how inventive or original – of the field of force of which they are a part. They will always want the redress of poetry to be an exercise of leverage on behalf of *their* point of view; they will require the entire weight of the thing to come down on their side of the scales. (*RP* 2)

In 'The Flight Path', Heaney is more bluntly direct in his refusal of the demands being placed upon him: ' "If I do write something, / Whatever it is, I'll be writing for myself." / And that was that.' (*SL* 25). Despite the finality of this last line, however, the concerns of the activist continue to intrude into the matter of the poem. The immediate next figure to appear in the piece is Ciaran Nugent, whose 'dirty protest' (refusing prison clothing and refusing to clean out his cell) served ultimately to initiate the campaign which would culminate in the hunger strike deaths of the early 1980s. As Nugent appears in the poem his 'red eyes' drill 'their way through . . . rhymes and images', boring their way, as it were, into Heaney's poetic project. The immediate task within which the shock of Nugent's gaze is registered is, appropriately enough, Heaney's translating of the Ugolino segment of Dante's *Inferno*. The translation had appeared in *Field Work* and Heaney quotes three lines of his own translation here:

> *When he had said all this, his eyes rolled*
> *And his teeth, like a dog's teeth clamping round a bone,*
> *Bit into the skull and again took hold.*
>
> (SL 25)

Ugolino's tale is one of self-consuming hatred. Imprisoned in a boarded-up room with his four children, he is forced to watch his offspring starve to death.[3] In hell, he exacts a bitter revenge on his jailer, Archbishop Ruggieri (Roger, in Heaney's translation) by biting into his skull. The bringing together of this narrative with the invocation of the figure of Nugent provides a peculiarly resonant image uniting hunger, hatred, and self-destruction in an intimate, endless, and unavailing cycle of revenge.

Section 4 of 'The Flight Path' is just one of several places in *The Spirit Level* where the present collapses into the past (either the literal past or the cultural past of literary reference) and, in common with many of Heaney's earlier poems, this collection is much troubled by 'revenants' – figures from beyond the grave who return to protest, interrogate, or bear witness. In 'Two Lorries', for instance, a deft account of a delicate flirtation between Agnew (the local coalman) and the poet's mother becomes inextricably intertwined with a narrative of the bombing of Magherafelt bus station. This intertwining is reinforced by Heaney's choice of the sestina form as a structuring device for the poem. The inwrought complexity of the format is registered by Neil Corcoran, who maps out its basic rules as follows: 'The sestina is an intricate form composed of six stanzas of six lines each, followed by an envoy of three lines, in all of which rhymes are replaced by end-words in a recurrent but shifting pattern; the envoy containing, in its three lines, all six end-words'.[4] Form contrives with content here to lace past and present together, so that Agnew and the poet's mother become locked into a kind of fractured indefinite present in which the respite and relief of continuous time is lost. In the wake of the explosion, the poet imagines his mother stranded in the bus station, her bags full of the ashes of destruction:

After that happened, I'd a vision of my mother,
A revenant on the bench where I would meet her
In that cold-floored waiting-room in Magherafelt,
Her shopping bags full up with shovelled ashes.

(*SL* 13–14)

'Keeping Going' too is haunted by revenants, summoned now
by one of the most basic of human acts:

Piss at the gable, the dead will congregate.
But separately. The women after dark,
Hunkering there a moment before bedtime.

(*SL* 11)

Seeing this dead congregation mass yet again in a Heaney poem
we might almost be tempted to wish that he had never read his
Virgil and seen Aeneas venture among the departed. But 'Keeping
Going' is, in fact, a complexly wrought poem. It struggles for a
balance that it hardly manages to achieve, setting itself precariously between qualified hope and blank despair. The poem
celebrates the endurance of Heaney's brother, Hugh, who has
remained in Northern Ireland, working the land that Heaney
himself might have been expected to inherit (as the eldest son),
had he not chosen to dig with pen rather than spade. As in the
case of 'Two Lorries', the poem folds the past and the present
into each other, intertwining childhood memories with the
contemporary world. As a child, Hugh had amused his siblings
by pretending to be a Scotsman playing the bagpipes, impro-
vising his outfit using an upended kitchen chair and a whitewash
brush. The brush which doubles in this game as a sporran is
also used routinely in a kind of annual ritual, to paint the walls
of the farm buildings with lime, effecting a restoration that has
a symbolic resonance, associated with the renewing capacities of
spring: 'all that worked like magic. / Where had we come from,
and what was this kingdom / We knew we'd been restored to?'.
Beneath the white expanse of the walls, however, lies a contrasting
strip, 'a tar border' which serves as 'a black divide'. 'Border'
has, of course, a very particular inflection in an Irish context, as
it points to the line of division between Northern Ireland and
the Republic – the line which the republican movement has
sought to erase from the map. The significance of the tar border
is marked (perhaps a little heavy-handedly) when it is described

by Heaney as being 'Like a freshly-opened, pungent, reeking trench' (*SL* 10).

Later in the poem, in the wake of the dead having congregated at the gable – presumably one of the walls whitewashed and bordered – we gain a full sense of what is implied in this ominous description. In the very town where Hugh lives out his life, a part-time member of the security forces is the victim of a leisurely political murder. His head is blasted against a whitewashed wall and, slumping in death, he falls 'past the tarred strip, / Feeding the gutter with his copious blood'. Here, the tar border that we have seen described as 'like a freshly opened . . . reeking trench' declines into an actual trench – the drain that carries away the reeking blood from the reservist's freshly opened wound. The murder tears through the fabric of the opening sections of the poem, which were filled with childish wonder and a sense of vernal hopefulness. Now another sense of 'whitewashing' comes to the surface in the poem – its colloquial sense of suppressing truth or hiding facts from consciousness or public view. The reservist's blood and brains are plastered across the white wall, where they become, at least for that moment, undeniable. And no amount of reimagining, no springtime rite of renewal can serve to offer reparation for – or can whitewash – this death.

In the final section of the poem, Heaney provides an image of his brother going about his daily business in the heart of the town where the murder has taken place: 'Your big tractor / Pulls up at the Diamond, you wave at people, / You shout and laugh above the revs'. But the poem is marked by a clear consciousness that quotidian life can never fully re-establish itself in the wake of what has happened. The poet says of his brother 'you cannot make the dead walk or right wrong'. At this point, the poem turns inward, interrogating the value of the quotidian world itself – even if it could ever be restored. Hugh is imagined steadying himself in a barn, struggling through an epileptic fit, and reviving again, resurfacing to the smell of excrement in a circumscribed world: 'coming to in the smell of dung again / And wondering, is this all? As it was / In the beginning, is now and shall be?' This is, for Heaney, an uncharacteristically bleak image of country life – even without the after-image of murder hanging in the air. The final lines of the poem offer a picture of resigned endurance: 'Then rubbing your eyes and seeing our old brush / Up on the byre door, and keeping going' (*SL* 12). In one sense, what we are hearing in these lines is the note of bleak resignation that we find so often in Samuel Beckett – as at the conclusion of *The Unnamable*, where the narrator brokenly accedes to the imperative of the narrative itself:

> you must go on, I can't go on, you must go on, I'll go on, you must say words, as long as there are any, until they find me, until they say me, strange pain, strange sin, you must go on, perhaps it's done already, perhaps they have said me already, perhaps they have carried me to the threshold of my story, before the door that opens on my own story, that would surprise me, if it opens, it will be I, it will be the silence, where I am, I don't know, I'll never know, in the silence you don't know, you must go on, I can't go on, I'll go on.[5]

But the closing lines of Heaney's poem also indicate a certain stubborn faith in the persisting, if compromised, powers of reimagining that were once available in childhood. The paint-brush still, Heaney seems to be insisting, has a certain potency and potential, even in a shattered world.

We can get a clearer sense of this dogged, compromised optimism, I would suggest, in the closing line of 'The Flight Path', where Heaney tells us that 'somewhere the dove rose. And kept on rising' (*SL* 26). This final assertion can be understood by referring back to the poem's opening, where Heaney's father makes a paper boat for him and, as he pulls at the paper folds to open the boat out, the poet tells us 'A dove rose in my breast'. This rising is matched, in the end of section 1, by a sinking prompted by the inutility of the boat's perfection:

> the little pyramid
> At the centre every bit as hollow
> As a part of me that sank because it knew
> The whole thing would go soggy once you launched it.
>
> (*SL* 22)

The transformation of the sheet of paper into a boat prompts a sense of elation, as it is a kind of small-scale marvel. But that sense of elation is tempered by the realization that the process of transformation is ultimately illusory – the boat will saturate and sink (like that hollow part of the speaker) because it remains a sheet of paper, not a boat. We might recall here William Carlos

Williams' anti-metaphorical poem 'The Term', in which a sheet of brown paper, blown by the wind in the street, assumes the form of a man and is hit by a passing car, but the poem ends

> Unlike
> a man it rose
> again rolling
>
> with the wind over
> and over to be as
> it was before.[6]

The closing line of Heaney's poem, however, refuses to be tethered to the drag of sinking realism – instead, it insistently hitches itself to the buoyancy of the initial upward movement that pledges faith in the possibility of transformation. At the end of 'The Flight Path' the dove rises and, crucially, keeps on rising, describing, in the process, something like a flight path of hopefulness.

This note of tempered hope is characteristic of many of the poems included in *The Spirit Level*, most obviously the case in 'The Gravel Walks', where Heaney challenges himself to 'walk on air against your better judgement' (*SL* 40), a lightsomeness echoed in 'The Swing', where the poet asserts that

> In spite of all, we sailed
> Beyond ourselves and over and above
> The rafters aching in our shoulderblades,
> The give and take of branches in our arms.
>
> (*SL* 49)

We also find poems here which provide a positive accommodation for the volume's persistent revenants. 'Damson', for instance, appears at first encounter to offer us a stereotypical Heaney vision of the interpenetration of the present and a ghost-ridden, nightmare-laden past. As the bricklayer works on the poet's childhood home, the stain of a damson fruit leaks through his lunchbag. As in the case of the tar strip in 'Keeping Going', the seeping redness is fraught with meaning, here explicitly signalled: 'Damson as omen, weird, a dream to read' (*SL* 15) ('weird' here having the double meaning of 'strange' and 'fateful' – as in *Macbeth*'s 'weird sisters'). The red stain is a portent that can be 'read' both forwards and backwards. It anticipates the wound that the bricklayer will accidentally inflict on himself in the course of his work, as it also anticipates the inevitable rent-a-revenant crew who faithfully appear in the second section of the poem, 'with their tongues out for a lick of blood / . . . crowding up the ladder all unhealed'. The poem slips predictably into classical mode, calling on the bricklayer to 'drive them off / Like Odysseus in Hades lashing out / With his sword'. Nothing much new in this, but as the poem draws to a close, we do find a new note entering, as Heaney brings himself to reject – or, at least, invert – the easy classical turn. In a move reminiscent of Williams, he uncouples the connection he had earlier established between the bricklayer and his classical precursor: 'But *not* like him – / Builder, not sacker, your shield the mortar board' (emphasis added). Unlike Odysseus, then, the bricklayer is a maker, not a destroyer, and this inversion persists to the end of the poem:

> Drive them back to the wine-dark taste of home,
> The smell of damsons simmering in a pot,
> Jam ladled thick and steaming down the sunlight.
>
> (*SL* 16)

The builder is enjoined here to turn the revenants back from their pursuit of blood into the pursuit of the homely actions of domestic life – cooking jam and ladling it into jars. In this way, the image of the damson too is recovered – freed from its initial ominous metaphorical freight. 'Wine-dark' is a telling descriptor here, as Homer persistently uses the formulation in phrases such as 'the wine-dark sea'. So, again, Heaney offers us an inversion of the classical, invoking not the wine-dark sea on which the warrior Greeks venture, but rather the domestic 'wine-dark taste of home'. As Neil Corcoran has observed, in these closing lines, '[t]he violently dead are removed from the damson of their blood to the damson of their previous, pacific domestic lives, and the figure has grief, tenderness, longing and the desperate desire for reparation in it all at once'.[7]

The note of hopeful liberation signalled here is matched in a number of other poems in *The Spirit Level*. Thus, while 'To a Dutch Potter in Ireland' – Heaney's translation from the Dutch of J. C. Bloem – is haunted by images of 'the terrible event' of the war, when the addressee of the poem 'Night after night . . . in the Netherlands, / . . . watched the bombers kill' (*SL* 3), the second section of the poem registers a different kind of life, 'After Liberation', as the title indicates. In this life 'the rye crop waves beside the ruins' and the addressee comes to realize that

> to wake and know
> Every time that it's gone and gone for good, the thing
> That nearly broke you –
> Is worth it all.

(SL 4)

The same note of emancipation sounds in 'Mint'. In this poem we encounter another gable, but, unlike 'Keeping Going', what we find at this house end is not a congregation of the departed, but rather a clump of fragrant herbs. The plant appears, unexpectedly, amongst the detritus of daily living, 'Growing wild at the gable of the house / Beyond where we dumped our refuse and old bottles'. Up to the point of its discovery, the mint has gone unnoticed, but now the poet takes it as a signal of 'promise / And newness', offering 'something callow yet tenacious'. It is 'callow' in the sense of being youthful and inexperienced – and thus to be nurtured – but also 'tenacious' in that it has clung on and endured, despite its unpromising location. Heaney celebrates the plant's endurance by proclaiming 'let all things go free that have survived' and he extends the plant's emancipation to all who, like prisoners, might be set free from bondage of one sort or another: 'Let the smells of mint go heady and defenceless / Like inmates liberated in that yard' (SL 6).

The Spirit Level, then, registers the anxieties of traditional conflicts and offers an anguished hope for the reimagining of conflictual paradigms. At the same time, it conceives of an emancipatory moment which might lie beyond conflict – 'after liberation', once the prison walls have crumbled. The motive force behind these thematics is not hard to find. The collection was published in 1996, and two years previously, in August 1994, the IRA (followed by the loyalist paramilitary groups) had announced a cessation of operations, to allow space for the British and Irish governments and the Northern Irish political parties – including the IRA's own political wing, Sinn Féin – to enter into negotiations in search of a wholly political solution to the Irish conflict. While the ceasefires were widely welcomed, they were also greeted with a certain degree of wariness. Previous initiatives of this kind had ended in failure. A 1972 ceasefire had seen a group of IRA leaders flown to London for direct contact with the British government; the group had included Martin McGuinness and Gerry Adams – two of the main Sinn

Féin negotiators involved in the peace process initiated by the 1994 ceasefire. The 1972 cessation was short-lived and was quickly followed by 'Bloody Friday', when the IRA set off 22 bombs in Belfast, killing 9 civilians and 2 British soldiers.

The 1994 ceasefire in its turn came to an end (in February 1996), in part owing to the inert intransigence of an embattled Conservative government in Britain, which was dragging its way through the fag-end of an over-extended period of rule. The ceasefire would be reinstated in July 1997, raising the possibility of real progress in the search for a political solution to the crisis. For *The Spirit Level*, however, all of these developments were still in the future and Heaney quietly and guardedly celebrated the original cessation of hostilities in the penultimate poem included in the volume – 'Tollund'. The poem takes its cue, obviously, from *Wintering Out*'s 'The Tollund Man' and it is conspicuously dated '*September 1994*' – a month after the original IRA ceasefire. Where, in the earlier poem, Heaney had anticipated 'Some day I will go to Aarhus' (*WO* 36), in the later poem he registers his fulfilment of that promise. But where 'The Tollund Man' could imagine only a symbolic, mythologized resolution of the Irish conflict, by the time the new poem came to be written, as Heaney says, 'Things had moved on'. And where the younger Heaney imagines that 'Out there in Jutland' he will 'feel lost, / Unhappy and at home', his older counterpart is altogether more sanguine and less desolate, finding himself 'footloose, at home beyond the tribe'. Standing with his companions he feels they are, collectively,

> More scouts than strangers, ghosts who'd walked abroad
> Unfazed by light, to make a new beginning
> And make a go of it, alive and sinning,
> Ourselves again, free-willed again, not bad.

> (*SL* 69)

They are 'scouts' in the sense that they have been sent, not into enemy territory, but into the unfamiliar territory of peace and resolution, where the ritual killings of the past have been submerged in a modern landscape, rendered 'user-friendly' for tourists. Again Heaney has recourse to his overworked image of revenancy, but here it is the living group to which he belongs (perhaps, by symbolic extension, the whole population of Northern Ireland) who are 'ghosts who'd walked abroad' and unlike his previous revenants, who occupy a classical tenebrous Hades, this group of ghosts are 'Unfazed by light' and, ultimately, prepared to make a new beginning, they are alive again – as if death has only been a temporary state. In the final line, 'Ourselves again' has a particular potency in an Irish context. The name of the IRA's political wing – Sinn Féin – translates into English as 'Ourselves Alone', pledging a dogged faith in an essential Irish identity and self reliance. At its most negative the racial ethic indicated in the name can suggest an obscurantist isolationism and an atavism that seeks to disjoin the Irish (or, at least, a certain segment of that community that could be nominated 'Irish') from fruitful contact with other communities. By cancelling the 'alone' and replacing it with 'again', Heaney suggests a kind of rebirth of Irishness and a breaking of traditional isolationist introversion. The final poem in *The Spirit Level* catches the same air of optimistic potential. Driving through the beautiful west of Ireland landscape, Heaney realizes that it is futile to think that he can stop and capture its force; he must move onward through it, experiencing the moment as it comes. He ends by imagining the impact which the unexpected may have on human consciousness, metaphorically rendered it as the crosswinds that might nudge against his car:

> You are neither here nor there,
> A hurry through which known and strange things pass
> As big soft buffetings come at the car sideways
> And catch the heart off guard and blow it open.
>
> (SL 70)

In a poem which has been quoted to the point of exhaustion during the course of the Irish conflict, 'The Stare's Nest by My Window', W. B. Yeats declared that

> We had fed the heart on fantasies,
> The heart's grown brutal from the fare;
> More substance in our enmities
> Than in our love.[8]

The poem does, however, seem peculiarly apt here.[9] 'The Stare's Nest' is one section of a longer poem, entitled 'Meditations in Time of Civil War', which was written in the aftermath of the Irish War of Independence, when former Irish allies disagreed over the terms of the autonomy deal being offered by the British government and began to fight each other in a short-lived, but bitter conflict. The ceasefires prompted similar internal wranglings, but what I want to register here is the contrast between Yeats's heart grown brutal and Heaney's heart caught off guard and blown open. 'Guardedness' has been a key principle in Irish thinking during the course of the conflict – as indicated neatly in the clichéd phrase which Heaney picks up on elsewhere, 'whatever you say, say nothing'. But here the heart is *off guard* and so finds itself opened outward; rendered receptive. We have noted before that the final poems of Heaney's books often have a particular significance, signalling thematic and poetic developments still on the horizon. Here we might say that the final word, as well as the final poem, of the collection has a special importance, since *The Spirit Level* is, precisely, 'open' to anticipated and desperately hoped for new political developments.

Having dwelt on the ending of *The Spirit Level*, we might turn back and consider what lies at the centre of that volume – the poem which Helen Vendler has described as the book's 'emotional centrepiece'.[10] 'Mycenae Lookout', Vendler suggests, has been written 'because it seemed the political troubles might be over, and one could write *finis* – with a summary sequence – to the whole incomprehensible slaughter'.[11] The conceit of the poem is drawn from Aeschylus's *Agamemnon*, which charts the return of its titular hero to Argos, following the sack of Troy, in the company of his lover, the Trojan visionary Cassandra. Both Agamemnon and Cassandra are murdered by Agamemnon's wife Clytemnestra and her lover Aegisthus. These murders – like many of those charted elsewhere by Heaney – are part of a greater extended cycle: Aegisthus is, in fact, Agamemnon's cousin, the only surviving child of Thyestes, whose other children were murdered, baked in a pie and served up to Thyestes by Agamemnon's father Atreus, in an act of revenge for Thyestes' having seduced his wife and disputed his right to reign in Argos. Clytemnestra's own rationale for killing her husband is in part driven by Agamemnon's having acceded to the sacrificial slaying of their daughter Iphigenia, during the early stages of the Trojan campaign. The extended story thus offers a tale of atrocity heaped on atrocity in a spiralling cycle of tragic revenge.

Heaney takes a peripheral character from Aeschylus's play, a watchman who serves as chorus and – rather in the manner of

Tom Stoppard's *Rosencrantz and Guildenstern are Dead* – places him at the very centre of the narrative. Neil Corcoran has identified the watchman as a figure for Heaney himself, noting that where the watchman characterizes himself as 'the lookout / The queen's command had posted and forgotten', in a poem entitled 'In the Beech', in the 'Sweeney Redivivus' section of *Station Island* (where Sweeney serves as a kind of alter ego for Heaney himself) the narrator also proclaims 'I was a lookout posted and forgotten' (*SI* 100).[12] What we find in the opening of 'Mycenae Lookout' is a kind of textual fingerprint of the poem's author, but, as Corcoran also notes, the filiations between Heaney and the unnamed lookout should be obvious anyway. Like Heaney, the lookout is a witness to horrifying events who feels both complicit in their horror and powerless in the face of that horror. He is spurred into articulation, even as he feels oppressed by the weight of that articulation and disgusted by its content:

> And then the ox would lurch against the gong
> And deaden it and I would feel my tongue
> Like the dropped gangplank of a cattle truck,
> Trampled and rattled, running piss and muck,
> All swimmy-trembly as the lick of fire,
> A victory beacon in an abattoir . . .
>
> (*SL* 29)

The lookout lives in silence with the betrayal of his master, as he hears the extravagant sexual groaning of Clytemnestra penetrating the floorboards up to where he keeps watch. In a segment of the poem reminiscent of *North*'s 'Punishment', he is a voyeur gawping at the distracted, charged figure of Cassandra, a prophet who foresees the ultimate desolation of the house of Atreus. Here Heaney is much more brutal and less equivocal than in the earlier poem – the effect of Cassandra's prophesy of doom is to inculcate a

> shock desire
> in bystanders
> to do it to her
>
> there and then.
> Little rent
> cunt of their guilt.
>
> (*SL* 32)

105

Where in *North*, the 'artesian' stanza had been used to drill down into the land in search of the wellsprings of the past, here the stanzaic form has a kind of brutal phallic quality to it, as if the lines themselves are perpetrating the rape that the bystanders fantasize, smashing the coherency of Cassandra's being. This is more explicit and more shocking than anything Heaney has previously attempted and it focuses in small savage compass the accumulated atrocities of conflict.

The death of Agamemnon – stabbed in his bath by Clytemnestra and Aegisthus – brings a further sense of complicit betrayal to the lookout, as he feels again that his silence renders him culpable:

> it was the king I sold.
> I moved beyond bad faith:
> for his bullion bars, his bonus
> was a rope-net and a blood-bath.

(SL 36)

But the outcome of the deaths of Agamemnon and Cassandra is that 'peace had come upon us'. It is an exhausted peace, bought at a terrible price. Furthermore, though the poem nowhere acknowledges it, the peace achieved is purely temporary. Though Heaney alludes to Cassandra's prophesy, he does not give her a voice explicitly to articulate it. In Aeschylus's play, foreseeing Agamemnon's death and her own, Cassandra predicts:

> We two
> must die, yet die not vengeless by the gods. For there
> shall come one to avenge us also, born to slay
> his mother, and to wreak death for his father's blood.
> Outlaw and wanderer, driven far from his own land,
> he will come back to cope these stones of inward hate.[13]

What Cassandra's prophecy points to is that Clytemnestra and Aegisthus will in turn be killed, by Clytemnestra and Agamemon's son Orestes, who will be driven from Argos by the Furies as a result of the killings. Finally, however, having been pursued through the world by the Furies, Orestes will be allowed to return to Argos, following the intervention of Athene.

Somewhere beneath the surface of Heaney's poem, then, may be a submerged (and, we might say, prophetic – in the manner of 'Docker') acknowledgement that the ceasefires in whose wake the poem is written are unlikely to mark the final endpoint of Ireland's own cycle of violence (we might note here that it was during the IRA's reinstated ceasefire that the worst single atrocity of the conflict occurred, when dissident republicans killed 29 people in the 1998 Omagh bombing). For all that, the concluding segment of the poem does attempt to celebrate the peace that has, for now, been achieved. The section opens with a beautifully still image – the filled bath, pure, translucent, and undisturbed. The stillness is broken by the warrior, who comes to the bath to wash away the blood of battle. As Helen Vendler notes, the poem here registers 'a trust that blood-letting can find water for its purification' (though, again, we might note that even this hopeful image must be tempered by the recollection that Agamemnon was, as we have seen, murdered in his bath).[14] In a return to a version of the positive artesian logic of the early poetry, Heaney extends the metaphor of water as a source of purification to an imaging of wells sunk into the ground, probing beyond contamination. Those who build the well-shaft return from it having learned something valuable, 'deeper in themselves for having been there' and the final image of the poem is of the sluicing fresh water itself 'in the bountiful round mouths of iron pumps / and gushing taps' (*SL* 37). We arrive back here, then, I would suggest, to the realm of the '*omphalos*', associated explicitly by Heaney in *Preoccupations* with the pumping of water from a pure source: 'The horses came home to it [the communal pump] in those first lengthening evenings of spring, and in a single draught emptied one bucket and then another as the man pumped and pumped, the plunger slugging up and down, *omphalos, omphalos, omphalos*' (*P*. 17). As Heaney himself registers in *Preoccupations*, the literal meaning of the Greek word is 'navel' and it is associated with 'the stone that marked the centre of the world' for the Greeks, located at Delphi. Drawing together the source of pure water, the omphalos, and the navel stone at Delphi, home of the Greek oracle, we might say that Heaney ends 'Mycenae Lookout' by imagining a parallel prophesy to Cassandra's, which conceives of a positive future, in which the cycle of atrocity and revenge can be broken. In contrast to previous such imaginings in Heaney, however, this time his aspiration is founded on more than just the machineries of mythology and ancient histories. In this instance, Heaney's visions have fruitfully intersected with the difficult, momentous and prosaic world of political negotiations and compromise.

What Heaney seems to be moving tentatively towards in many of the poems included in *The Spirit Level* is, then, a faith in the invocation that he offered in another of his classically inspired texts: his version of Sophocles' *Philoctetes*, published under the title *The Cure at Troy* in 1990. Heaney ends the play by foregrounding another Chorus figure, who (rather in the manner of Prospero's epilogue in Shakespeare's *Tempest*) steps out of the frame of the narrative to offer a petition that directly addresses contemporary concerns, speaking of the anguish of 'A hunger-striker's father' and 'The police widow in veils'. The Chorus tells us that

> History says, *Don't hope*
> *On this side of the grave.*
> But then, once in a lifetime
> The longed-for tidal wave
> Of justice can rise up,
> And hope and history rhyme.
>
> So hope for a great sea-change
> On the far side of revenge.
> Believe that a further shore
> Is reachable from here.
> Believe in miracles
> And cures and healing wells.
>
> (CT 77)

Heaney's adroit conceit of hope and history rhyming was much quoted during the course of the Northern Irish peace process – to the extent that it achieved the same kind of clichéd status as Yeats's 'heart grown brutal'.[15] Nevertheless, we might say that the 'healing wells' imagined here resonate with the 'iron pumps' and 'gushing taps' of 'Mycenae Lookout'. And the concluding lines of the Chorus's metadramatic speech in *Cure* seem in retrospect once again curiously prophetic:

> If there's fire on the mountain
> Or lightning and storm
> And a god speaks from the sky
>
> That means someone is hearing
> The outcry and the birth-cry
> Of new life at its term.
>
> (CT 78)

By the end of the decade which *The Cure at Troy* opened, it was beginning to seem as if the 'birth-cry' of a new political life was indeed reaching its term in Ireland.

The possibility of a significant shift in the political paradigms which stagnantly governed Irish life throughout most of Heaney's career opens the way for a reimagining of models of identity, so that 'Irishness' as a concept can be opened up to interrogation, and identity politics in general can be more closely examined. Such interrogation and re-examination is peculiarly relevant to a figure such as Heaney. Though his 'Irishness' has been foregrounded by commentators (including, of course, the present writer), and though he has to a large extent collaborated in this foregrounding, Heaney nevertheless is very clearly someone who has not been bound by geographical accidents of birth (as, we might say, 'Keeping Going' suggests that his brother Hugh has been). '[B]e advised / My passport's green. / No glass of ours was ever raised / To toast *The Queen*' (*OL* 88), Heaney writes in *An Open Letter*, but that Irish passport (now a wine-dark European Community burgundy) has been much used by Heaney in worldwide travel and he has held prestigious appointments at Oxford and at Harvard. Heaney's position as Professor of Poetry at Oxford served on occasion, as we have already seen, as a source of conflict for him. While hunger strikers were dying in Ireland, Heaney was enjoying the hospitality of the British establishment. But Heaney's complex relationship with Britain runs deeper than this – and certainly deeper than his throw-away line about not toasting the British Queen would indicate. Heaney is steeped in the writing of the English Renaissance, with quotations from and references to a wide variety of the writers of this period – including Thomas Wyatt, Edmund Spenser, Walter Ralegh, William Shakespeare – continuously surfacing in his work. While Heaney sometimes offers a critical engagement with these writers – with both Spenser and Ralegh appearing in his poetry as emblematic figures of English imperialism – he also accepts the literary inheritance which these writers offer, drawing on their work itself and on the forms and poetic conventions which they helped to establish. Additionally, we might note that Heaney's major works have always been published by the London-based firm of Faber and Faber and his books have sold widely in Britain. Heaney was being tipped to succeed Ted Hughes as

British Poet Laureate, before word filtered through the media that he had privately made it clear that he would not accept the post, if offered.

Despite what a concentration on his position as a member of the minority nationalist-minded Catholic community in Northern Ireland might suggest, Heaney's canon does include a number of poems that acknowledge the contingent complexities of identity and that reject the view of a traditional form of nationalism conceiving of national identity as fixed and easily determined. In *The Haw Lantern*'s 'Terminus', for example, Heaney registers the fact that he 'grew up in between', at the intersection of several different worlds, and he makes the implications of this clear in his Nobel Lecture, 'Crediting Poetry', where he observes that '[w]ithout needing to be theoretically instructed, consciousness quickly realizes that it is the site of variously contending discourses' (*OG* 451–2). In the same piece, he gives a flavour of some of these contending discourses from his own childhood experience:

> I would climb up on an arm of our big sofa to get my ear closer to the wireless speaker . . . what I was after was the thrill of story, such as a detective serial about a British special agent called Dick Barton or perhaps a radio adaptation of one of Capt. W. E. Johns's adventure tales about an RAF flying ace called Biggles. . . . [I]n that intent proximity to the dial I grew familiar with the names of foreign stations, with Leipzig and Oslo and Stuttgart and Warsaw and, of course, with Stockholm. (*OG* 448–9)

In *Field Work*, Heaney provides an emblematic instance of such cultural flux and indetermination in the figure of Francis Ledwidge, an Irish poet killed fighting as a British soldier in France during the First World War, in 1917. For Heaney, Ledwidge is a 'dead enigma', a Catholic who was partly sympathetic to the militant nationalist cause (he contributed to a volume of poems published to raise money for the dependants of those imprisoned after the 1916 uprising in Ireland), who fought beside fervently engaged Ulster Protestants and, having survived the Dardanelles, was killed in the third battle of Ypres.[16] The complexity of Ledwidge's position is captured in an understated manner by Heaney's insistent references to the Boyne, the river which runs through the Boyne valley and flows on through Drogheda, where Ledwidge is imagined 'court[ing] at the seaside'

(*FW* 60). Quoted in the poem, Ledwidge says 'My soul is by the Boyne, cutting new meadows', but the Boyne, of course, has clear historical resonances in an Irish context, as it was at the Battle of the Boyne in 1690 that the Catholic Irish, who had aligned themselves with the British king James II, were comprehensively beaten by a Protestant army led by William of Orange – a victory celebrated to this day in Ireland by unionists. Ledwidge is in every sense, therefore, located at the crossing point of several lines of British and Irish identity. In his poem, Heaney imagines this overlapped set of identifiers as failing to achieve any kind of useful balance: 'In you, our dead enigma, all the strains / Criss-cross in useless equilibrium'. It is of little consolation here that a kind of reconciliation is achieved in death, where Ledwidge consorts with his Protestant Irish fellow-soldiers who have suffered the same fate as himself, death, as ever, being a great leveller.

Though Heaney finds in this poem that the crossed inscriptions of identity lead only to fragmentation and contradictoriness, he returns to identitarian themes at later points in his writing career, to more positive effect. A second emblematic figure of cultural flux is considered by Heaney in *The Haw Lantern*'s 'Terminus', identified as 'the last earl on horseback in midstream / Still parleying, in earshot of his peers' (*HL* 5). The reference here is to Hugh O'Neill (*c.* 1540–1616), a fascinating figure from Irish history, who has attracted the attention of the playwright Brian Friel (and, earlier, of the Irish writer Seán Ó Faoláin) as well as of Heaney himself.[17] O'Neill was a curiously liminal figure, who moved easily among the different worlds of sixteenth-century Ireland. He was fostered by an English settler family near Dublin and made several trips to the court of Elizabeth I (Spenser's 'Faerie Queene') while a young man. He eventually returned to his native Ulster, where he contrived to succeed both to the traditional native Irish title of 'The O'Neill' and to the British aristocratic title 'Earl of Tyrone'. Ultimately, O'Neill proved intractable as a servant of the crown and he fought an extended and complexly conceived campaign against Elizabeth's forces in Ireland.

'Terminus' refers to an incident in 1599, when O'Neill encountered the Earl of Essex, who had been sent to Ireland by Elizabeth with an enormous army, in the expectation that he would bring

O'Neill to submission (the despatch of Essex's army is noted in the opening lines of the final act of Shakespeare's *Henry V*). O'Neill's and Essex's forces finally encountered each other at Bellaclinthe and O'Neill requested a private meeting with Essex at a nearby river. A contemporary account by a member of the Essex party tells us that

> Knowing the foorde, [O'Neill] found a place, where he, standing up to the horsses belly, might be neere enough to be heard by the L. Liuetenant, though he kept the harde grownde; upon which notice the L. Liuetenant drew a troupe of horsse to the hill above the foord, and seing Tirone theare alone, went doune alone: at whose comming Tirone saluted his [Lordship] with a greate deale of reverence, and they talked neere half an houre, and after went ether of them up to their compagnies on the hills.[18]

The outcome of the meeting was that O'Neill persuaded Essex to institute a truce and to withdraw his forces. Essex eventually returned to England, where he was severely taken to task by the queen.

O'Neill, as this anecdote indicates, was a strikingly mercurial figure. Known to the English as an Irish 'arch rebel', he nevertheless approaches Essex in his own terms, employing the elaborate ceremonial practices of chivalry in a series of persuasive gestures, which serve, in a multiple sense, to disarm his English opponents. The place of his parley with Essex is deftly chosen: he locates himself at the centre of a ford, a crossing point between the opposite banks of a river. From this middle ground between opposing sides, he uses his facility with the cultures of both Ireland and England to defuse the anticipated and much-trumpeted hostilities. The appeal of this historical vignette to Heaney should be obvious. Professionally, we might say, Heaney has always operated a kind of poetic version of 'shuttle diplomacy' between the opposing banks of the Irish Sea. Like O'Neill, Heaney moves within high cultural and political realms in both Ireland and Britain; he too is perfectly familiar with the contrasting manoeuvrings and engagements that will be efficacious in either culture (we recall, for instance, the common decency of his relapsed '*naw*'s and '*aye*'s in 'Clearances' IV [*HL* 28]). And perhaps at a grander level, he may hope for the possibility that he might be able to use his cross-cultural licence to effect some kind of pacific understanding between the two cultures.

112

History indicates, of course, that O'Neill could not manage to juggle identities to his own advantage indefinitely. He met a sterner opponent in Essex's successor, Charles Blount, who comprehensively routed the Irish forces at the Battle of Kinsale in 1601, with O'Neill eventually being pushed into continental exile in 1607. But Heaney, I would suggest, continues to meditate on the question of crossed identities and the potentials which may be sprung from them. His most concerted engagement with the issue comes in 'Frontiers of Writing', the final lecture included in *The Redress of Poetry*, published just a year after the 1994 IRA ceasefire. Here Heaney offers a figure which he dubs the 'quincunx', a geometry of five fortified buildings dotted around the island of Ireland, all with historical and literary associations. The initial four buildings of the quincunx are: (i) an imagined originary Irish tower, located somewhere in the centre of the island; (ii) Kilcolman Castle, the colonial home of the English poet Edmund Spenser, whose relationship with Ireland and the Irish was a troubled mixture of repulsion and grudging attraction; (iii) Thoor Ballylee, the Norman tower in Co. Clare in the west of Ireland, occupied by W. B. Yeats, the Protestant poet who helped to foster cultural nationalism in Ireland; (iv) the Martello tower on the east coast, near Dublin, briefly occupied by James Joyce and used by him as the opening location for *Ulysses*, which, in a manner familiar from Heaney himself, seeks to intertwine Irish culture fruitfully with the heritage of the classical past. Heaney sees these four cultural structures as being related to each other as follows:

> Spenser's tower faces in to the round tower of the mythic first Irish place and sees popery, barbarism and the Dark Ages; Yeats's tower faces it and sees a possible unity of being, an Irish nation retrieved and enabled by a repossession of its Gaelic heritage; Joyce's tower faces it and sees an archetypal symbol, the *omphalos*, the navel of a reinvented order, or maybe the ivory tower from which the chaste maid of Irish Catholic provincialism must be liberated into the secular freedoms of Europe. (*RP* 199–200)

The crucial final link in this structure for Heaney is Carrickfergus Castle, which he associates with the poet Louis MacNeice, another fascinatingly liminal figure, who was born in Belfast in 1907, but whose Protestant family originally came from Connemara in the west of Ireland. In a memoir of his childhood, MacNeice described Connemara as a 'dream world' and observed that 'The West of Ireland' was

> a phrase which still stirs me, if not like a trumpet, like a fiddle half heard through a cattle fair. My parents came from that West or, more precisely, from Connemara, and it was obvious that both of them vastly preferred it to Ulster. The very name Connemara seemed too rich for an ordinary place. It appeared to be a country of windswept open spaces and mountains blazing with whins and seas that were never quiet, with drowned palaces beneath them, and seals and eagles and turf smoke and cottagers who were always laughing and who gave you milk when you asked for a glass of water.[19]

MacNeice's vision of the west is a touch misty-eyed and idealized (if self-consciously so, perhaps), but the crucial aspect of his life that Heaney wants to stress is that, even as his Irish identity is complexly formed (as an Ulster Protestant with deep affiliations with the traditionally Catholic west) that identity is further intertwined with a set of connections with England, as MacNeice was educated at the English public school, Marlborough, from where he went on to study at Oxford, and he spent most of his working life in England (a good deal of it as an employee of the BBC). MacNeice himself realized the complexity of all of this and in section XVI of his extended poem, *Autumn Journal*, he produced a deeply conflicted meditation on his relationship to both Irish and English identity. He is scathingly critical of the hypocrisies of republican and unionist alike, but his willingness wholly to embrace an English identity is blocked by a feeling that certain values still persist in Ireland that have long since atrophied in England:

> Such was my country and I thought I was well
>   Out of it, educated and domiciled in England,
> Though yet her name keeps ringing like a bell
>   In an under-water belfry.
> Why do we like being Irish? Partly because
>   It gives us a hold on the sentimental English
> As members of a world that never was,
>   Baptised with fairy water;
> And partly because Ireland is small enough,
>   To be still thought of with a family feeling,
> And because the waves are rough

114

That split her from a more commercial culture;
And because one feels that here at least one can
  Do local work which is not at the world's mercy
And that on this tiny stage with luck a man
  Might see the end of one particular action.[20]

This upbeat note is not sustained by MacNeice (the very next line of the poem is 'It is all self-deception of course'), but this section of his poem closes with a tense balancing of what he finds both thoroughly depressing and exasperatingly appealing about Ireland:

Send her no more fantasy, no more longings which
  Are under a fatal tariff.
For common sense is the vogue
  And she gives her children neither sense nor money
Who slouch around the world with a gesture and a brogue
  And a faggot of useless memories.[21]

There is a certain priggishness of tone in MacNeice here, but what he has to say is none the less searingly valid for all that. It is the balance of forces manifest in MacNeice's career that Heaney finds attractive and it is for this reason that he makes Carrickfergus Castle the final, completing element of the quincunx. MacNeice, for Heaney

by his English domicile and his civil learning is an aspect of Spenser, by his ancestral and affectionate links with Connemara an aspect of Yeats and by his mythic and European consciousness an aspect of Joyce. ... He can be regarded as an Irish Protestant writer with Anglocentric attitudes who managed to be faithful to his Ulster inheritance, his Irish affections and his English predilections. As such, he offers a way in and a way out not only for the northern Unionist imagination in relation to some sort of integral Ireland but also for the southern Irish imagination in relation to the partitioned north. (*RP* 200)

As is often the case in his critical writings, Heaney's imagination here plays on MacNeice so that the historical poet is to some extent remoulded to fit the context of his successor's schema. The awkward corners of MacNeice's brilliant truculence are worn away so that he can more neatly fit in the round hole of Heaney's analysis. But Heaney's aim is a laudable one: to conceive of a figure which might allow the imagination to 'fly the nets' (as

Joyce's Stephen Dedalus would have it) of static, isolationist identity ('ourselves alone'), opening out culture and identity to the embracing of difference and indeterminacy. What Heaney attempts to plot here is what he characterizes, in a striking phrase adopted from John Montague, as 'an escape route from . . . "the partitioned intellect" ' (*B*. xxv). Politically, Heaney argues in his Nobel Lecture, the outcome of this reimagining might be that the mark of partition – the border which separates the two segments of the island of Ireland – will also be reimagined, and he expresses the hope that that partition might

> become a bit more like the net on a tennis court, a demarcation allowing for agile give-and-take, for encounter and contending, prefiguring a future where the vitality that flowed in the beginning from those bracing words 'enemy' and 'allies' might finally derive from a less binary and altogether less binding vocabulary. (*OG* 461)

At the same time as Heaney was working through these notions of multiplicitous identity and the rearticulation of partition, he was also working on translating the Old English poem *Beowulf* into contemporary English. The motivations energizing this undertaking are complex, but they are – in some respects at least – directly related to the project we have just been charting. A previous translator of the poem, Michael Alexander, has characterized *Beowulf* as 'a sort of a dinosaur [mounted] in the entrance hall of English Literature'.[22] Heaney's grappling with this dinosaur can be seen as a bold gesture of poetic appropriation. Many years ago, the literary critic Harold Bloom proposed a theory of literary history which suggested that 'strong' poets engaged in a kind of fraught oedipal struggle with their literary predecessors.[23] Heaney, as we have repeatedly seen, is very conscious of his poetic ancestors – his work is consistently saturated both with classical references and with references to the high cultural English poetic tradition. His characteristic strategy for encountering his predecessors is, we might say, to assimilate them into his own work, by quotation and by adaptation. In translating *Beowulf* Heaney is, in a sense, seeking to absorb into his own canon one of the seminal and central early poems of the field of English literature. In addition to its significance in a poetic context, Heaney's gesture of mastering *Beowulf* also has a very definite political edge to it. The Irish poet's translation is accented by the idiom and vocabulary of his own native Co. Derry – we hear Unferth warn Beowulf 'this time you'll be worsted' (*B*. 18; *worsted* meaning beaten, or got the better of), while the narrator comments of Unferth that, following Beowulf's victory, 'There was ... / less of his blather' (*B*. 31; idle talk), and we hear of a 'bawn' (*B*. 18; fortified dwelling), a 'brehon' (*B*. 48; a judge), 'graith' (*B*. 94; ready). It is something of a strange business, when a translation requires a further layer of translating gloss to render it wholly intelligible to the average speaker of the language into which the translation has been made, but we can see that part of what is motivating Heaney here is a desire to set the stamp of his own culture on this monument of English literature. In this manner, the translation becomes a kind of postcolonial gesture – an audacious seizing of a central metropolitan cultural space in the name of the culture of the inferiorized colony. Rather in the manner of *Station Island*'s 'Widgeon', where a man plucking the feathers from a mutilated dead bird finds its voicebox and, blowing through it, produces 'unexpectedly / his own small widgeon cries' (*SI* 48), in translating *Beowulf* Heaney vocalizes through the poem 'a familiar local voice, one that had belonged to relatives of my father, people whom I had once described (punning on their surname) as "big-voiced scullions" ' (*B*. xxvi). The voice of the English epic thus becomes an Irish voice.

There is also, however, something more complex at play here, which returns us to the aspirations set out by Heaney in 'Frontiers of Writing' and in 'Crediting Poetry'. In his Introduction to *Beowulf*, Heaney makes clear that, for him, translating the poem is not just a matter of setting his own mark on this canonical text; it also involves recognizing cultural roots that, previously, he might have preferred to suppress. Heaney notices, for instance, that, unconsciously, an early poem such as 'Digging' has much, structurally, in common with Anglo-Saxon poetry. He notes that the opening lines of the poem 'were made up of two balancing halves, each half containing two stressed syllables' and that 'in the case of the second line there was alliteration linking "digging" and "down" across the caesura' (*B*. xxiii). Thus, as Heaney comes to recognize, '[p]art of [him] ... had been writing Anglo-Saxon from the start'. So Heaney feels able to claim *Beowulf* as, in some sense, his own – 'I consider *Beowulf* to be part of my voice-right', he says – but, in another sense, we might say that that recognition involves a parallel acknowledgement of the interpenetrability of cultures within the islands of Britain and Ireland, an acknowledgement of the fact that these cultures are not mutually exclusive binary opposites. Heaney himself registers this shift in his thinking about language (and, by extension, about culture more generally):

> I tended to conceive of English and Irish as adversarial tongues, as either/or conditions rather than both/and, and this was an attitude that for a long time hampered the development of a more confident and creative way of dealing with the whole vexed question – the question, that is, of the relationship between nationality, language, history and literary tradition in Ireland. (B. xxiii)

We can see, then, some of the issues involved in the business of translating for Heaney. But we might also ask what it is about the poem's actual content that might have made it attractive to him. There are some connections here that can be traced back to his other major translation, *Sweeney Astray*, a version of the traditional Irish poem *Buile Suibhne*. Both books locate themselves at the cusp of cultural change – the Irish poem directly addressing the shift between pagan culture and Christianity in Ireland, the Anglo-Saxon looking back to a prior pagan age from a later Christian vantage point. As Michael Alexander observes in relation to *Beowulf*,

> Unlike his heroes, the poet is Christian, and the cosmology and aetiology are largely Christianized. A typical Anglo-Saxon moralist, his traditional gnomic gravity and wryness are modified in places by a Christian note of agonized moral and spiritual concern such as we find in the homilies of the time.[24]

The clash of the two cultures is registered in *Beowulf*, when the narrator tells us dismissively of the Danes' fidelity to pagan deities, as they 'vowed / offerings to idols':

> That was their way,
> their heathenish hope; deep in their hearts
> they remembered hell. The Almighty Judge
> of good deeds and bad, the Lord God,
> Head of the Heavens and High King of the World,
> was unknown to them.
>
> (B. 8)

As in the case of *Buile Suibhne*, where pagan and Christian ethics collide, Alexander notes a conflict in the *Beowulf* poet's handling of his material – a tension between a desire to celebrate the heroic and a Christian repugnance at the consequences of the unrelenting martial code which underpins the heroic: 'the poet makes *Beowulf* more of an elegy than a celebration of heroic life, partly because he laments the passing of the heroic virtue of his martial ancestors, partly because he has a horror of war such as might be felt in a settled community in an insecure age'. Alexander's vision of the original Anglo-Saxon poet might also be said to apply to Heaney as the poem's most recent translator. While the poem does, indeed, celebrate the heroic, foregrounding Beowulf's three great martial contests, it is also shot through with a sense of the grinding inevitability of conflict in a society which privileges antagonism and heroism above all else. As Heaney observes in his introduction:

> All conceive of themselves as hooped within the great wheel of necessity, in thrall to a code of loyalty and bravery, bound to seek glory in the eye of the warrior world. The little nations are grouped around their lord; the greater nations spoil for war and menace the little ones; a lord dies, defencelessness ensues; the enemy strikes; vengeance for the dead becomes an ethic for the living, bloodshed begets further bloodshed; the wheel turns, the generations tread and tread and tread. (*B.* xiv)

Ultimately, we might say, the poem recognizes the futility of this way of life. The warrior who buries the golden hoard protected by the dragon does so because his entire society has been wiped out:

> My own people
> have been ruined in war; one by one
> they went down to death, looked their last
> on sweet life in the hall. I am left with nobody
> to bear a sword or burnish plated goblets,
> put a sheen on the cup.
>
> (*B.* 71–2)

'Pillage and slaughter', he bitterly observes, 'have emptied the earth of entire peoples' (*B.* 72) and his observation is an anticipation of the fate of Beowulf's own people, the Geats, who likewise, in the years following Beowulf's death, will be ground-down and annihilated, as a mourner at the hero's funeral predicts:

A Geat woman too sang out in grief;
with hair bound up, she unburdened herself
of her worst fears, a wild litany
of nightmare and lament: her nation invaded,
enemies on the rampage, bodies in piles,
slavery and abasement. Heaven swallowed the smoke.

(B. 98)

Within this violent culture, whole civilizations can be swallowed up like the smoke from Beowulf's pyre.

The alternative to such grinding, cyclical destruction is, Heaney suggests in his Introduction, an acknowledgement of past history and a willingness to reimagine history's potential. In closing his Introduction, Heaney invokes one of his own poems, 'The Settle Bed', from *Seeing Things*. This poem celebrates an inheritance which Heaney received from an elderly relative – an old-fashioned, cumbersome bed. Heaney only managed to fit the bed into one of the rooms of the Glanmore cottage with great difficulty and he associates the bed's stolid implacability with an Ulster temperament common to Catholic and Protestant alike. But the key point for Heaney is that the bed *can be* accommodated to a new environment, brought to meet the needs of a new generation and, as such, the bed becomes emblematic of history, of culture, and of politics. 'Whatever is given', he tells us,

Can always be reimagined, however four-square,
Plank-thick, hull-stupid and out of its time
It happens to be.

(ST 29)

The poem closes with the figure of a lookout, but this one differs from the sombre, traumatized and guilt-ridden Mycenae lookout of *The Spirit Level*. In 'The Settle Bed' the lookout is a 'far-seeing joker' who, posted high on the mast of a fog-bound ship, 'declared by the time that he had got himself down / The actual ship had been stolen away from beneath him' (ST 29). It is hard to tell when the fog of entrenched antagonism might lift in Ireland. We might say, however, that one of the enduring values of Heaney's poetry has been his willingness to imagine unexpected destinations for the hull-stupid ship of history.

Appendix: A Brief Sketch of Irish History

The islands of Britain and Ireland lie adjacent to each other, and so their histories have always been complexly intertwined. Over the centuries there has been a considerable amount of migration back and forth between the two islands. In 1167 the Irish petty king Diarmait MacMurchada sought help in an internecine feud from the English king Henry II. This occasioned an Anglo-Norman incursion into Ireland and a large part of the island of Ireland came under English dominion as a result. Over the course of the next three centuries or so the area over which the English securely ruled gradually declined and many of the original settler families became 'hibernicized', adopting Irish customs, the Irish language, and the Irish system of law.

In the sixteenth century, various attempts were made to revivify England's presence in Ireland, frequently leading to war as the Irish resisted. When the English church broke with the church of Rome during the course of the Reformation in the sixteenth century, the majority of the Irish remained Catholic, so effecting an important distinction between the two populations. By the end of the sixteenth century the Irish leader Hugh O'Neill was at the head of an anti-English coalition which aimed, with the help of support from catholic Spain, either to break or radically to reconfigure the link with England. Ironically, O'Neill had originally been sponsored by the English themselves and had visited the court of the English monarch several times. O'Neill was finally defeated and was forced into exile in 1607. His power-base had been in the northern Irish province of Ulster and the plan to impose control on this region included the assignment of large swathes of Ulster land to loyal subjects from Britain.

By this point the English throne had passed to the Scottish king James VI, who reigned as James I in England and who sought to unify the island of Britain into a single kingdom. Under the settlement plan, a large amount of Ulster land was assigned to Scottish settlers – the ancestors of many of the Protestant families living in the north of Ireland today.

Despite O'Neill's defeat, attempts to challenge the British presence in Ireland continued. The Irish situation intersected with upheavals in Britain in the middle decades of the seventeenth century. In 1649 Oliver Cromwell, whose anti-monarchical parliamentarians had triumphed in Britain, arrived in Ireland and set about reducing the Irish to subservience. The severity of Cromwell's campaign – during the course of which he wiped out the populations of several towns which resisted him – has remained a potent memory in Ireland. At the end of the seventeenth century, Ireland once again became intertwined in British politics, when the Catholic Irish supported the Catholic king James II, whose accession to the throne was opposed by British Protestants. One of the principal battles of this war was fought in Ireland, when a coalition of Catholic forces under James was defeated by a coalition of Protestant forces led by William of Orange, who acceded to the English throne as William III. This battle occurred at the Boyne valley in 1690 and it proved a defining (and enduring) moment for Protestant identity in Ireland.

Protestant victory at the end of the seventeenth century led to the introduction of increasingly stringent measures against Catholics over the course of the eighteenth century. These measures were relaxed somewhat as the century drew to a close, but the French revolution of 1789 inspired a radical movement in Ireland which included a fragile coalition of Catholics and Protestants. The movement which grew out of this was called the 'United Irishmen' and this group staged a short-lived uprising in 1798. Though the group was unsuccessful, many present-day militant republicans trace their roots back to the United Irishmen and their leader, Theobald Wolfe Tone. One of the main results of the uprising was that the Irish parliament (which had only ever had limited powers and a very narrowly based electorate) was abolished and Ireland was incorporated into a United Kingdom with Britain in 1801.

Agitation to secure Catholic rights continued throughout the nineteenth century, in parallel with efforts to restore some form of Irish legislative autonomy. In 1845 disease was detected in the Irish potato crop and for the next several years the crop failed, with catastrophic results. The Irish peasantry relied on potatoes (which could be grown abundantly on small patches of even quite poor land) as their staple diet. The failure of the crop led to widespread famine, with somewhere in the region of one million people dying of starvation. A further one million emigrated. The scale of these numbers indicates that the British were insufficiently energetic in their response to the crisis and this served to compound Irish bitterness towards the link with Britain. Anti-British militancy began to flourish in the second half of the nineteenth century, under the name of 'Fenianism'. At the same time, a less radical movement emerged with the aim of securing 'Home Rule' for Ireland by constitutional means. The focal point for the Home Rule movement was the parliamentarian Charles Stewart Parnell. The rise of the movement was warily viewed by Ulster Protestants, who feared Catholic ascendancy, and it fuelled a 'unionist' or 'loyalist' militancy to match its republican counterpart.

The Home Rule movement foundered for a number of reasons. Parnell's popularity declined after he was named as the third party in a divorce action; unionist opposition became more organized, more vocal, and more determinedly militant; and the First World War intervened. In 1916, amid much confusion, militant republicans staged an uprising, proclaiming Ireland a republic and declaring that the link with Britain was henceforth severed. The timing of the uprising was symbolic: the action was initiated at Easter weekend and the leaders of the uprising drew heavily on Catholic symbolism of blood sacrifice and renewal. The insurrectionary forces were quickly defeated, but the British erred tactically by killing the leaders in a series of executions lasting some nine days, thus garnering support for the militant separatist agenda. In elections for the British parliament held in 1918 republican candidates, standing as members of the Sinn Féin ('Ourselves Alone') party (founded in 1907) swept the board, taking 73 of 105 seats (unionists took 26 seats; the remainder went to the Irish Parliamentary Party). Sinn Féin boycotted the British parliament and set up their own alternative assembly in Ireland (the *Dáil*), which the British authorities declared illegal. By 1920 violence was becoming widespread, as republican militants attacked British forces, who responded in kind, often with great ferocity. In the following year, the Ulster Unionists, in a pre-emptive strike against the possibility of Irish independence, secured a quasi-autonomous status for Ulster within the United Kingdom and a unionist-dominated Ulster parliament was opened by George V.

In 1921 republican and British forces agreed to a truce and the British government offered the Irish a treaty which included limited independence (as a 'Free State') for 26 counties of Ireland, partitioning off 6 of Ulster's 9 counties, to continue as a quasi-autonomous region within the UK. The treaty was approved by the Dáil by a narrow margin (64 in favour, 57 against). The sticking point for those who opposed the treaty was, generally, partition, and the opponents of the settlement split from their former allies to fight a civil war, with the intention of securing a pact which included all of the island of Ireland within the independence settlement. The war was bitterly fought and served to divide Irish society – and many Irish families – for decades to come. By 1923 the pro-treaty forces had prevailed and the new state gradually settled down to self-governance. In 1937, a new constitution was approved by parliament and in 1948 the free state was declared a republic (Ireland left the Commonwealth in the following year).

As the new Irish state took shape, it was clear that the country was dominated by a determinedly (and, many felt, oppressive) Catholic ethos. This ethos was enshrined in the 1937 constitution, which acknowledged the 'special position' of the Catholic church in Ireland and which, in keeping with Catholic teaching, outlawed divorce. These developments were warily observed by Protestants in the Northern Ireland statelet, not least because the constitution symbolically laid claim to Irish jurisdiction over the entire island of Ireland, not just the 26 counties. Partly in response to this, unionists in Northern Ireland exploited their privileged status of having a guaranteed majority in the Northern Irish parliament to concentrate power in their own hands at the expense of Catholics, who were discriminated against in housing, employment, and education. By a process of gerrymandering Catholics were sometimes deprived of political power even in those areas where they were in a majority.

While both states established their partisan, introverted contours, republican militancy rumbled on sporadically decade by decade. These militants, concentrated in the Irish Republican Army (IRA), dedicated themselves to ending partition and achieving a 'united Ireland'. By the end of the 1960s, however, the organization was largely moribund. A new generation of Irish Catholic activists did emerge at this time, many of whom had gained access to higher education as a result of the broadening of the educational franchise by the postwar Labour government in Britain. These activists were inspired by the Civil Rights movement in the US and they pressed for an end to discrimination in areas of life such as housing and employment. Originally conceived as a non-partisan movement, the civil rights agenda quickly became enmeshed in the larger issue of partition. Civil rights protesters were opposed with great force by the Northern Irish authorities and by militant loyalist gangs, in part because they saw civil rights as a Trojan horse for those seeking a united Ireland. The situation quickly degenerated and disaffection among nationalist-minded Northern Irish Catholics prompted the resurgence of the IRA, who initiated a renewed campaign dedicated to ending partition and completely severing the link with Britain. By 1969, British troops had been deployed on the streets of Northern Ireland and in 1972 the British government suspended the Northern Irish parliament, bringing control of the region back fully within the remit of the British parliament at Westminster. In this same year British soldiers shot dead thirteen unarmed civil rights protesters, thus confirming, in the eyes of many nationalists, the partisan nature of the British intervention in Northern Irish affairs.

Over the course of the next three decades, the situation went from bad to worse, with repeated murders, bombings, and low-level 'ethnic cleansing'. Atrocities were perpetrated on all sides, serving to harden attitudes still further. By the early 1990s, however, channels of communication had opened up between militant republicans and the British government. A complex process of negotiation, involving the British and Irish governments and politicians from both sides of the divide in Northern Ireland led to the IRA declaring a cessation of hostilities in August 1994. The IRA ended this cessation in February 1996, by detonating a one tonne bomb in London, killing two people, but a further ceasefire was negotiated, which came into force in July 1997. This ceasefire made space for the evolution of a peace deal, which was signed by the two governments and the majority of Northern Ireland's parties in April 1998. Implementation of this deal has proved to be slow and deeply problematic, but it did result in the handing back of power to a Northern Irish assembly at the end of 1999, with the devolved executive consisting of elected representatives drawn from all communities in Northern Ireland. The deal envisages that Northern Ireland will retain its autonomous status within the United Kingdom, but that there will be stronger official ties with the Irish Republic and that structures will be evolved to reinforce ties between Ireland and the UK as a whole. It remains to be seen whether this deal will indeed have created the foundation for a durable peace.

Notes

INTRODUCTION

1. Patrick Kavanagh, *Collected Poems* (London, 1972), xiii.
2. For those less well versed in the details of the conflict in Northern Ireland, I have included a very short survey of the history of the conflict as an appendix to this volume. Please note that this appendix is not intended to be anything other than a very broadly sketched and condensed overview; readers who require a more detailed account should consult some of the works listed in the Further Reading Section of the Select Bibliography.
3. W. B. Yeats, *Collected Poems* (London, 1982), 243.
4. In weighing the responsibilities of the poet, Heaney aligns himself with the Russian poet Osip Mandelstam as much as with Yeats. See GT 71–90.
5. Yeats, *Collected Poems*, 151. See also the next poem in the collection: 'An Irish Airman Foresees His Death'.

CHAPTER 1. 'LIVING ROOTS AWAKEN IN MY HEAD': PLACE AND DISPLACEMENT

1. For a discussion of Heaney's work by Hobsbaum, see 'Craft and Technique in *Wintering Out*', in Tony Curtis (ed.), *The Art of Seamus Heaney* (Bridgend, Wales, 1982; third edition, 1994), 35–43.
2. On the relationship between Heaney's work and that of Ted Hughes, see Neil Rhodes, '"Bridegrooms to the Goddess": Hughes, Heaney and the Elizabethans', in Mark Thornton Burnett and Ramona Wray (eds), *Shakespeare and Ireland: History, Politics, Culture* (Basingstoke, 1997), 152–72. On Heaney and another near contemporary, Philip Larkin, see John Wilson Foster, *The Achievement of Seamus Heaney* (Dublin, 1995), 20. Heaney himself discusses the influence of Hopkins on his early work in 'Feeling into Words', in *Preoccupations*.
3. Neil Corcoran, *A Student's Guide to Seamus Heaney* (London, 1986), 44.

4. Interview with John Haffenden in Haffenden's *Viewpoints* (London, 1981), 65.

5. Andrew Waterman, 'The best way out is always through', in Elmer Andrews (ed.), *Seamus Heaney: A Collection of Critical Essays* (London, 1992), 12.

6. Heaney's gesture here is not unlike that of Yeats when, addressing his ancestors in his preface to *Responsibilities*, he writes: 'Although I have come close on forty-nine, | I have no child, I have nothing but a book, | Nothing but that to prove your blood and mine' (*Collected Poems* (London, 1982), 113).

7. Helen Vendler, *Seamus Heaney* (London, 1998), 21. Heaney himself has also registered an opposing effect of his upbringing, namely that 'some part' of him 'is entirely unimpressed by the activity [of writing], that doesn't like it, but it's the generations, I suppose of rural ancestors – not illiterate, but not literary. They, in me, or I through them, don't give a damn' (Haffenden interview, 63).

8. In his poems on childhood and familial conflict Heaney is greatly influenced by the US poet Theodore Roethke. See, in particular, Roethke's *The Lost Son and Other Poems*, included in *The Collected Poems of Theodore Roethke* (London, 1966).

9. Michael Parker, *Seamus Heaney: The Making of the Poet* (London, 1993), 66.

10. Patricia Coughlan, ' "Bog Queens": The Representation of Women in the Poetry of John Montague and Seamus Heaney', in Toni O'Brien Johnson and David Cairns (eds.), *Gender in Irish Writing* (Milton Keynes, 1991), 99.

11. Patrick Kavanagh, *Collected Poems* (London, 1972), 136.

12. Seamus Heaney, 'Kavanagh of the Parish', *Listener*, 26 Apr. 1979, 577.

13. Homer, *The Iliad*, trans. Robert Fitzgerald (New York, 1975), bk. 18, ll. 554–9.

14. Philip Sidney, *A Defence of Poetry* (Oxford, 1966), 24. See Robert Welch, ' "A rich young man leaving everything he had": Poetic Freedom in Seamus Heaney', in Andrews (ed.), *Seamus Heaney*, 151–2.

15. Henry Hart, *Seamus Heaney: Poet of Contrary Progressions* (New York, 1992), 61. John Kerrigan usefully contrasts Heaney with fellow Northern Irish poet Ciarán Carson in this regard, observing that 'Carson's attitude to names ... has an anti-Heaneyesque edge; his mock etymological earnestness does not find meaning in a bog but discovers a swamp in philology' (John Kerrigan, 'Earth Writing: Seamus Heaney and Ciarán Carson', *Essays in Criticism*, 48/2 (1998), 159).

16. Neil Corcoran, *The Poetry of Seamus Heaney: A Critical Study* (London, 1998), 44.

17. Place-names have a particular kind of political history in Ireland, indicative of the island's colonial past. Some native Irish place-names survive in their original form, but many others – like 'Anahorish' – were anglicized by the colonists, thus erasing their original meaning value. In other cases, the Irish name has been completely lost, having been replaced by an unrelated new English name. For an interesting dramatization of such issues of naming, see Brian Friel's play *Translations*.
18. Corcoran, *Poetry*, 43.
19. Corcoran, *Student's Guide*, 90.
20. I am presuming that 'riverback', in the 1993 edition of *Wintering Out*, is a typographical error. *New Selected Poems* gives what I take to be the correct 'riverbank' (25).
21. Kerrigan, 'Earth Writing', 148.
22. John Wilson Foster has observed that 'Heaney has always intended his poetry to be, and indeed it is, a political poetry of considerable if oblique power' (*Achievement*, 53).

CHAPTER 2. 'WHERE THE FAULT IS OPENING': POLITICS AND MYTHOLOGY

1. Neil Corcoran notes in *The Poetry of Seamus Heaney: A Critical Study* (London, 1998) that 'the reading matter of [Heaney's] childhood included, along with English comics and adventure stories, such Irish nationalist publications as the *Wolfe Tone Annual*, with its celebrations of the 1798 rebellion and its contemporary significance' (238).
2. Interview with Seamus Deane, 'Unhappy and at Home', *Crane Bag*, 1/1 (1977), 5.
3. Michael Parker, *Seamus Heaney: The Making of the Poet* (London, 1993), 95.
4. Edmund Spenser, *A View of the Present State of Ireland*, in R. Morris (ed.), *The Complete Works of Edmund Spenser* (London, 1869), 654.
5. Karl Marx, *The Eighteenth Brumaire of Louis Bonaparte*, in Robert C. Tucker (ed.), *The Marx–Engels Reader* (New York, 1978), 594.
6. Parker, *Seamus Heaney*, 106.
7. John Haffenden, *Viewpoints* (London, 1981), 60.
8. Quoted in Neil Corcoran, *A Student's Guide to Seamus Heaney* (London, 1986), 96
9. Ibid. 78.
10. Bernard O'Donoghue, *Seamus Heaney and the Language of Poetry* (Hemel Hempstead, 1994), 6.
11. Heaney in an interview with Harriet Cooke, quoted in Corcoran, *Student's Guide*, 95.

12. See Parker, *Seamus Heaney*, 131. Parker draws on Heaney's commentary for a 1980 BBC film entitled *The Boyne Valley*, directed by David Hammond.
13. R. F. Foster, *Modern Ireland, 1600–1972* (London, 1989), 142.
14. Conor Cruise O'Brien, 'A Slow North-east Wind: Review of *North*', reproduced in Michael Allen (ed.), *Seamus Heaney* (Basingstoke, 1997), 26.
15. Blake Morrison, *Seamus Heaney* (London, 1982), 68.
16. Here Heaney has much in common with a writer such as Chinua Achebe, whose *Things Fall Apart* (its title derived, of course, from Yeats's 'The Second Coming') charts the destruction of native cultures as European colonialism advances across the African continent.

CHAPTER 3. 'I HEAR AGAIN THE SURE CONFUSING DRUM': REVERSIONS AND REVISIONS

1. Neil Rhodes, '"Bridgrooms to the Goddess": Hughes, Heaney and the Elizabethans', in Mark Thornton Burnett and Ramona Wray (eds), *Shakespeare and Ireland: History, Politics, Culture* (Basingstoke, 1997). John Kerrigan also interestingly discusses the variant versions of the poem in 'Hand and Foot', *London Review of Books*, 27 May 1999, 20. I'm very grateful to Dr Kerrigan for providing me with a copy of this piece.
2. James Simmons, 'The Trouble with Seamus', in Elmer Andrews (ed.), *Seamus Heaney: A Collection of Critical Essays*, 59.
3. Edna Longley, *Poetry in the Wars* (Newcastle, 1986), 185. Longley has refined this observation in her more recent *The Living Stream: Literature and Revisionism in Ireland* (Newcastle, 1994), in which she observes: 'by politics I meant predatory ideologies, fixed agendas and fixed expectations' (9).
4. Desmond Fennell, *Whatever You Say, Say Nothing* (Dublin, 1991), 16–17. Fennell's own political location may be worth registering here. He has long indicated support for a frankly partisan nationalist reading of Irish history, castigating 'revisionist' historians who (in their own partisan way) have sought to interrogate the traditional verities of a nationalist historiography. See, for example, Fennell's 'Against Revisionism', in Ciarán Brady (ed.), *Interpreting Irish History: The Debate on Historical Revisionism* (Dublin, 1994).
5. Ciarán Carson, 'Escaped from the Massacre?', *Honest Ulsterman*, 50 (Winter 1975). For an excellent cross-reading between the work of Heaney and of Carson, see John Kerrigan, 'Earth Writing: Seamus Heaney and Ciarán Carson', *Essays in Criticism*, 48/2 (1998).
6. David Lloyd, *Anomalous States: Irish Writing and the Post-Colonial Moment* (Dublin, 1993), 27. Lloyd's chapter on Heaney in *Anomalous*

States is also included in Andrews (ed.), *Seamus Heaney*.

7. Heaney's sense of mythology and of the relationship between myth and history is also rather more complex than writers such as Carson and Lloyd allow. Heaney's views are in part informed by Richard Kearney's *Myth and Motherland* (included in *Ireland's Field Day* (Notre Dame, Ind., 1986)), which sets out a sophisticated reading of the relationship between history and mythology.

8. Seamus Deane, 'Talk with Seamus Heaney', *New York Times Review*, 84/48 (1979), 48.

9. Maurice Harmon, '"We Pine for Ceremony": Ritual and Reality in the Poetry of Seamus Heaney, 1965–75', in Andrews (ed.), *Seamus Heaney*, 76.

10. It is notable that in 'Incertus', from the 1975 collection *Stations*, Heaney uses the same phrase in relation to his own early writing: 'Oh yes, I crept before I walked' (*OG* 91). 'Incertus' was the pseudonym under which he published his earliest poems.

11. Neil Corcoran, *The Poetry of Seamus Heaney: A Critical Study* (London, 1998), 97.

12. See Michael Parker, *Seamus Heaney: The Making of the Poet* (London, 1993), 162.

13. Dante, *The Divine Comedy 2: Purgatorio*, trans. John D. Sinclair (Oxford, 1961), 25.

14. John Haffenden, *Viewpoints* (London, 1981), 60.

15. Neil Corcoran, *A Student's Guide to Seamus Heaney* (London, 1986), 163.

16. Corcoran, *Poetry*, 147.

17. Ibid. 136.

18. Helen Vendler, *Seamus Heaney* (London, 1998), 133.

CHAPTER 4. 'IT WAS MARVELLOUS AND ACTUAL': FAMILIARITY AND FANTASY

1. Quoted in Neil Corcoran, *A Student's Guide to Seamus Heaney* (London, 1986), 128.

2. *Collected Poems of Sir Thomas Wyatt*, ed. Kenneth Muir (Cambridge, Mass., 1950), 28.

3. *Selected Poems and Prefaces by William Wordsworth*, ed. Jack Stillinger (Boston, 1965), 108. Neil Corcoran has registered the profound impact of Wordsworth on Heaney's early career, observing of many of the poems in *Death of a Naturalist* that they 'are, as it were, written in the margin of such passages as the boat-stealing episode in Book I of *The Prelude*' – Neil Corcoran, *The Poetry of Seamus Heaney: A Critical Study* (London, 1998), 5.

4. Blake Morrison, *And When Did You Last See Your Father?* (London, 1994), 191, 198.

5. Corcoran, *Poetry*, 184.

6. See, for example, Corcoran, *Poetry*, 111; Henry Hart, *Seamus Heaney: Poet of Contrary Progressions* (New York, 1992), 152; John Foster Wilson, *The Achievement of Seamus Heaney* (Dublin, 1995), 41.

7. Yeats also writes about this clash of cultures, in taking up the traditional story of an imagined encounter between the dying mythical Celtic hero Oisín and St Patrick, who is said to have brought the Christian faith to Ireland. See his 'Wanderings of Oisin'.

8. *The Compact Edition of the Oxford English Dictionary* (Oxford, 1971), 689.

9. Helen Vendler, *Seamus Heaney* (London, 1998), 101.

10. *OED*, 765.

11. Vendler, *Seamus Heaney*, 136.

12. Henry Hart, 'What is Heaney Seeing in *Seeing Things*?', *Colby Quarterly*, 30/1 (Mar. 1994), 33.

13. Wilson, *Achievement*, 49.

CHAPTER 5. 'OURSELVES AGAIN, FREE-WILLED AGAIN, NOT BAD': THE UNPARTITIONED INTELLECT

1. Peter McDonald, *Mistaken Identities: Poetry and Northern Ireland* (Oxford, 1997), 14.

2. Neil Corcoran, *The Poetry of Seamus Heaney: A Critical Study* (London, 1998), 192.

3. In fact, historically, he was locked up with his two adult children and two grandchildren – Dante heightens the dramatic effect by making it four young children.

4. Corcoran, *Poetry*, 196. Corcoran continues at pp. 196–9 interestingly to discuss Heaney's use of the sestina and the significance of the variations he introduces into the form.

5. Samuel Beckett, *The Unnamable* in *The Beckett Trilogy* (London, 1979), 381–2.

6. S. Walton Litz and Christopher MacGowan (eds), *The Collected Poems of William Carlos Williams* (Manchester, 1987), vol. I, 452.

7. Corcoran, *Poetry*, 195.

8. W. B. Yeats, *Collected Poems* (London, 1982), 230–1.

9. Heaney himself quotes from this poem in his Nobel lecture, 'Crediting Poetry', where he observes that 'I have heard this poem repeated often, in whole and in part, by people in Ireland over the past twenty-five years' – see *OG*, 463–4.

10. Helen Vendler, *Seamus Heaney* (London, 1998), 156.

11. Ibid. 169.

12. Corcoran, *Poetry*, 191.

13. Aeschylus, *Oresteia*, trans. by Richard Lattimore (Chicago, 1953), 76.

14. Vendler, *Seamus Heaney*, 173.

15. Though, again, it might be said that Heaney himself retained a sense of the value of the lines, beyond their hardening into cliché. Invited to discuss the Irish situation on the UK's *Channel 4 News* on the night when the Northern Irish powersharing executive first met, Heaney closed the interview by reading this passage from *The Cure at Troy.*

16. For these details, see Michael Parker, *Seamus Heaney: The Making of the Poet* (London, 1993), 174–6.

17. See Friel's play *Making History* (London, 1989) and Ó Faoláin's novelized biography *The Great O'Neill* (London, 1942). Both writers have been taken to task by historians for their romanticized treatment of their subject. I have written about O'Neill at some length in chapter 4 of my *But the Irish Sea Betwixt Us: Ireland, Colonialism, & Renaissance Literature* (Lexington, KY, 1999).

18. Harrington, John, *Nugæ Antiquæ* (London, 1804), 299.

19. Louis MacNeice, *The Strings are False: An Unfinished Autobiography* (London, 1965), 216–17.

20. Louis MacNeice, *Collected Poems* (London, 1966), 132–3.

21. Ibid. 134.

22. *Beowulf*, trans. Michael Alexander (London, 1973), 10.

23. Harold Bloom, *The Anxiety of Influence: A Theory of Poetry* (Oxford, 1975).

24. Alexander (trans.), *Beowulf*, 29.

Select Bibliography

WORKS BY SEAMUS HEANEY

Death of a Naturalist (London: Faber & Faber, 1966).
A Lough Neagh Sequence (Manchester: Phoenix Pamphlet Poets, 1966).
Door into the Dark (London: Faber & Faber, 1969).
Wintering Out (London: Faber & Faber, 1972).
Soundings (Belfast: Blackstaff, 1972).
Stations (Belfast: Ulsterman, 1975).
Bog Poems (London: Rainbow, 1975).
North (London: Faber & Faber, 1975).
Field Work (London: Faber & Faber, 1979).
Preoccupations: Selected Prose 1968–1978 (London: Faber & Faber, 1980).
Selected Poems 1965–1975 (London: Faber & Faber, 1980).
The Rattle Bag: An Anthology of Poetry, as editor, with Ted Hughes (London: Faber & Faber, 1982).
An Open Letter (Derry: Field Day, 1983; repr. in *Ireland's Field Day*, Notre Dame, Ind. 1986).
Sweeney Astray (Derry: Field Day, 1983; London: Faber & Faber, 1984).
Station Island (London: Faber & Faber, 1984).
Hailstones (Dublin: Gallery, 1985).
Clearances (Dublin: Cornamona, 1986).
The Haw Lantern (London: Faber & Faber, 1987).
The Government of the Tongue: The 1986 T. S. Eliot Memorial Lectures and Other Critical Writings (London: Faber & Faber, 1988).
The Cure at Troy: A Version of Sophocles' Philoctetes (London: Faber & Faber, 1990).
The Tree-Clock (Belfast: Linen Hall Library, 1990).
New Selected Poems 1966–1987 (London: Faber & Faber, 1990).
Seeing Things (London: Faber & Faber, 1991).
The Redress of Poetry (London: Faber & Faber, 1995).
The Spirit Level (London: Faber & Faber, 1996).
Opened Ground: Poems 1966–1996 (London: Faber & Faber, 1998).
Beowulf (London: Faber & Faber, 1999).

INTERVIEWS

In excess of twenty-five interviews with the poet have been published. Major interviews include:

Brandes, Rand, *Salmagundi*, 80 (Fall 1988).
Cooke, Harriet, *Irish Times*, 28 Dec. 1973.
Deane, Seamus, 'Unhappy and at Home', *Crane Bag*, 1/1 (1977).
— 'Talk', *New York Times Book Review*, 2 Dec. 1979.
Druce, Robert, 'A Raindrop on a Thorn', *Dutch Quarterly Review*, 9 (1978).
Haffenden, John, 'Meeting Seamus Heaney', *London Magazine* (June 1979).
— Interview included in John Haffenden, *Viewpoints* (London, 1981).
Kinahan, Frank, *Critical Inquiry*, 8/3 (Spring 1982).
Randall, James, 'An Interview with Seamus Heaney', *Ploughshares*, 5/3 (1979).

CRITICAL STUDIES

For a short survey of Heaney scholarship, see Rand Brandes's extremely useful brief history of Heaney reception, 'Secondary Sources: A Gloss on the Critical Reception of Seamus Heaney 1965–1993', in the *Colby Quarterly* issue listed below.

Books

Neil Corcoran's book (originally published in 1986 as *A Student's Guide to Seamus Heaney*, then reissued in 1998 in an updated and expanded second edition under the title *The Poetry of Seamus Heaney*) remains the best all-round study of Heaney's work. Michael Parker's book is an indispensable guide to Heaney's biography (though it is also more than this, as Parker includes astute readings of the poems as well). Bernard O'Donoghue provides the best analysis of Heaney's language and poetics. Michael Allen's collection provides an excellent anthology of important Heaney criticism.

Michael Allen (ed.), *Seamus Heaney* (Basingstoke, 1997).
Andrews, Elmer, *The Poetry of Seamus Heaney: All in the Realms of Whisper* (London, 1989).
— (ed.), *Seamus Heaney: A Collection of Critical Essays* (London, 1992).
Bloom, Harold (ed.), *Seamus Heaney* (New York, 1986).
Corcoran, Neil, *A Student's Guide to Seamus Heaney* (London, 1986).
— *The Poetry of Seamus Heaney: A Critical Guide* (London, 1998).
Curtis, Tony (ed.), *The Art of Seamus Heaney* (3rd edn., Bridgend, Wales, 1994).

Foster, John Wilson, *The Achievement of Seamus Heaney* (Dublin, 1995).

Hart, Henry, *Seamus Heaney: Poet of Contrary Progressions* (New York, 1992).

Morrison, Blake, *Seamus Heaney* (London, 1982).

O'Donoghue, Bernard, *Seamus Heaney and the Language of Poetry* (Hemel Hempstead, 1994).

Parker, Michael, *Seamus Heaney: The Making of the Poet* (London, 1993).

Vendler, Helen, *Seamus Heaney* (London, 1998).

Articles

An enormous number of articles on Heaney have been published over the years. The following offers no more than a flavour of some useful recent criticism.

Allison, Jonathan, 'Acts of Union: Seamus Heaney's Tropes of Sex and Marriage', *Éire-Ireland*, 27/4 (1992). An interesting commentary on Heaney's marriage imagery, set usefully within the context of notions of political union.

Carson, Ciarán, 'Escaped from the Massacre?', *Honest Ulsterman*, 50 (Winter 1975). A telling and astute review of *North* by a fellow Northern Irish poet, who takes Heaney to task for political imprecision.

Colby Quarterly, 30/1 (Mar. 1994). This is a special issue of *Colby Quarterly* dedicated to Heaney's work. It contains Rand Brandes's review of Heaney reception from 1965 to 1993, as well as very interesting articles by Henry Hart (on *Seeing Things*) and Elizabeth Butler Cullingford.

Coughlan, Patricia, ' "Bog Queens": The Representation of Women in the Poetry of John Montague and Seamus Heaney', in Toni O'Brien Johnson and David Cairns (eds.), *Gender in Irish Writing* (Milton Keynes, 1991). An interesting feminist critique of Heaney's use of gendered imagery and metaphors.

Cullingford, Elizabeth Butler, 'Thinking of Her . . . as . . . Ireland: Yeats, Pearse, and Heaney', *Textual Practice*, 4/1 (Spring 1990). A useful commentary on the intersection between nationalism and gender.

Deane, Seamus, 'Seamus Heaney: The Timorous and the Bold', in *Celtic Revivals* (London, 1985). An assessment of Heaney's work by his friend and fellow Field Day director.

Fennell, Desmond, *Whatever You Say, Say Nothing* (Dublin, 1991). A pamphlet attacking Heaney as a poet who has courted popularity with international audiences without offering anything of real substance in his poetry. The piece is rather lightweight and is belligerent in a crudely personal way, but nevertheless does offer some cogent criticism of Heaney's work and what might be called 'the Heaney phenomenon'.

Kerrigan, John, 'Earth Writing: Seamus Heaney and Ciarán Carson', *Essays in Criticism*, 482 (1998). A very useful cross reading of these two Ulster poets.

Longley, Edna, 'Poetry and Politics in Northern Ireland', in *Poetry in the Wars* (Newcastle, UK, 1986). Part of this chapter is devoted to an examination of the politics of Heaney's poetry, especially as expressed in *North*. Longley, who might broadly be said not to be sympathetic to the nationalist political agenda, offers a useful and interesting critique of Heaney's political stance.

Rhodes, Neil, '"Bridegrooms to the Goddess": Hughes, Heaney and the Elizabethans', in Mark Thornton Burnett and Ramona Wray (eds), *Shakespeare and Ireland: History, Politics, Culture* (Basingstoke, 1997). An excellent comparison of Heaney and Hughes in the context of Renaissance literature.

Smith, Stan, 'The Distance Between', in Neil Corcoran (ed.), *The Chosen Ground: Essays on Contemporary Poetry in Northern Ireland* (Bridgend, Wales, 1992). A cogent, theoretically informed assessment of Heaney's recent poetry.

Wills, Clair, 'Language Politics, Narrative, Political Violence', *Oxford Literary Review*, 13/1–2 (1991). A sophisticated article on the politics of Heaney's language, with includes a useful interrogation of Heaney's use of gender.

FURTHER READING

The literary context

Brown, Terence, *Northern Voices: Poets from Ulster* (Dublin, 1975).

— *Ireland's Literature: Selected Essays* (Mullingar, Ireland, 1989).

Deane, Seamus, *Celtic Revivals* (London, 1985).

— *A Short History of Irish Literature* (London, 1986).

Dunn, Douglas, (ed.), *Two Decades of Irish Writing* (Manchester, 1975).

Longley, Edna, *Poetry in the Wars* (Newcastle, 1986).

— *The Living Stream: Literature and Revisionism in Ireland* (Newcastle, 1994).

Lloyd, David, *Anomalous States: Irish Writing and the Post-Colonial Moment* (Dublin, 1993).

McDonald, Peter, *Mistaken Identities: Poetry and Northern Ireland* (Oxford, 1997).

The historical and political context

Cairns, David, and Shaun Richards, *Writing Ireland: Colonialism, Nationalism and Culture* (Manchester, 1988). A survey of English writing on the subject of Ireland.

Coogan, Tim Pat, *The IRA* (rev. edn., London, 1995). A standard account of the militant Irish nationalist movement.

— *The Troubles: Ireland's Ordeal 1966–1995 and the Search for Peace* (London, 1995). An account of the most recent decades of the Anglo-Irish conflict.

Curtis, Liz, *Nothing but the Same Old Story: The Roots of Anti-Irish Racism* (London, 1985). A short history of English attitudes towards the Irish.

Devlin, Bernadette, *The Price of my Soul* (London, 1969). An autobiographical account of the early days of the Northern Irish Civil Rights movement by a Derry activist who served for a time as Member of Parliament for Derry.

Edwards, Ruth Dudley, *The Faithful Tribe: An Intimate Portrait of the Loyal Institutions* (London, 1999). A critical, but sympathetic, account of the protestant, unionist 'Orange Order'.

Farrell, Michael, *Northern Ireland: The Orange State* (London, 1980). A comprehensive history of the Northern Irish state, told from a socialist, nationalist perspective.

Foster, R. F., *Modern Ireland: 1600–1972* (London, 1989). A good, single-volume history of Ireland from the seventeenth to the twentieth centuries.

— *Paddy and Mr. Punch: Connections in Irish and English History* (London, 1993). A collection of essays on culture and history in an Anglo-Irish context.

Ireland's Field Day (Notre Dame, Ind., 1986). A selection of the first group of pamphlets on Irish political and cultural topics published by the Field Day Company, of which Heaney is a director. Includes Heaney's 'An Open Letter'.

McCann, Eamonn, *War and an Irish Town* (rev. edn., London, 1993). A personal account of life in Derry during the Civil Rights era, by a fellow ex-pupil of Heaney's secondary school.

Taylor, Peter, *Provos: Sinn Féin and the IRA* (London, 1997). This volume and the one that follows provide a portrait of the republican and loyalist militant movements, based on extensive interviews with key players in each case.

— *Loyalists* (London, 1999).

Index

Adams, Gerry, 101
Aegisthus, 104–108
Aeneas, 82, 89–90
Aengus, 42
Aeschylus
    Agamemnon, 104–108
Agamemnon, 104–108
Alexander, Michael, 116, 118–119
Alighieri, Dante, 76
    Divine Comedy, 62, 64, 89–90,
    95
Amnesty International, 71
Anchises, 82
Antaeus, 48
Aran Islands, 17–18
Armstrong, Sean, 61

Beckett, Samuel
    The Unnamable, 98
Belfast, 61, 93–94, 102
'Belfast Group', 8
Bloem, J. C., 100
Bloody Friday, 102
Bloody Sunday, 59–60, 125
Bloom, Harold, 116
Boyne, 42–43, 110–111, 122
Buile Suibhne, 72, 85–87, 118–119

Carlingford, 43
Carleton, William, 67
Carrickfergus Castle, 113, 115
Carson, Ciarán, 51–52, 56, 70
Cassandra, 104–108

Catholicism, 65–67
Civil Rights movement, 30, 59,
    125
Clonmacnoise, 90–91
Clytemnestra, 104–108
Corcoran, Neil, 10, 23, 26, 39, 60,
    66, 71–72, 85, 93, 95, 100, 105
Coughlan, Patricia, 17
Cromwell, Oliver, 122

Deane, Seamus, 53
Dedalus, Stephen, 116
Derrygarve, 25
Dinnseanchas, 23–26, 34
Donnelley, Brian, 38

Easter Rising, 32–33, 123
Essex, Earl of, 111–112
Ewart-Biggs, Christopher, 57

Faber & Faber, 8, 109
Famine, 31–32, 37–38, 123
Fennell, Desmond, 51, 54, 70
Foster, John Wilson, 91
Foster, R. F., 42
Friel, Brian, 73, 111

George V, 124
Glanmore, 73–77, 120
Glob, P. V., 39, 45
    The Bog People, 34, 38,
    42–43
Gunnar, 43